PRACTICE BOOK

VOYAGES
IN ENGLISH
GRAMMAR AND WRITING

5

LOYOLAPRESS.

Cover Design: Judine O'Shea
Cover Art: Pablo Bernasconi
Interior Design: Think Book Works
Editor: Pamela Jennett

ISBN-13: 978-0-8294-2830-8
ISBN-10: 0-8294-2830-5

LOYOLA PRESS.
3441 N. Ashland Avenue
Chicago, Illinois 60657
(800) 621-1008
www.loyolapress.com

Courier Companies / Kendallville, IN, USA / 03-15 / 4th Printing

Contents

GRAMMAR

Tips for Daily Maintenance

Dear Student:

The Daily Maintenance is a daily exercise that allows you to practice grammar skills you have already learned. Recall these tips as you complete each Daily Maintenance set:

- First, read the sentence and all the questions in the set.
- Think carefully about what will answer each question: Will the answer be the name of a part of speech? Will you need to identify a particular word from the sentence?
- Identify the parts of speech used in the sentence.
- Recall what you have previously learned about grammar.
- Write answers first for any questions you find easy.
- Once you have answered all the items you can, diagram the sentence. Diagramming helps you see how the parts of a sentence work together. A diagram might help you figure out the answers you don't know.
- Remember to work neatly as you write your answers and draw the diagram.
- If you are still unsure of an answer, use what you know to write the best answer you can.
- Read over your answers carefully.
- Check that you have written an answer for each question.
- Check that you have spelled words correctly.
- When your teacher reviews the answers, listen attentively and ask questions if something is unclear. Be sure to pay close attention to the questions that you had trouble answering. What you find out today may appear on the next day's Daily Maintenance set.

The Daily Maintenance allows you to check your progress in the grammar skills you are studying this year. It can help you figure out where you need to focus your energy. By using these tips and monitoring your own progress, you can master grammar skills for your grade. With practice, grammar skills will become second nature, and your writing will be stronger.

SECTION 1 | Daily Maintenance

1.1 **Ana chops the vegetables.**
   1. Which word is a proper noun?
   2. Which noun is plural?
   3. What word is a verb?
   4. Diagram the sentence here.

Ana
vegtables
chops

1.2 **The boys feed the tiny mice.**
   1. Is *boys* a common noun or a proper noun?
   2. Is the verb present tense or past tense?
   3. Which word is an irregular plural noun?
   4. Diagram the sentence here.

1.3 **We bought two hamburgers.**
   1. Is *We* a noun or a pronoun?
   2. Is *We* singular or plural?
   3. Is *two* used as an adjective or a noun?
   4. Diagram the sentence here.

1.4 **Nick counted the silver coins.**
   1. Which word is a singular noun?
   2. Is the verb regular or irregular?
   3. Which word is an adjective?
   4. Diagram the sentence here.

1.5 **Joann sent me a postcard.**
1. Is the verb regular or irregular?
2. What is the direct object?
3. Is *me* a noun or a pronoun?
4. Diagram the sentence here.

_____
_____
_____

1.6 **They are famous athletes.**
1. Which word is a subject pronoun?
2. Which word is a verb?
3. Is the verb an action verb or a linking verb?
4. Diagram the sentence here.

_____
_____
_____

1.7 **He gave her a beautiful bracelet.**
1. Is the verb present tense or past tense?
2. Which word is an object pronoun?
3. Which word is an adjective?
4. Diagram the sentence here.

_____
_____
_____

1.8 **Jenny tells us scary stories.**
1. Is the pronoun singular or plural?
2. Is the plural noun regular or irregular?
3. What part of speech is *scary*?
4. Diagram the sentence here.

_____
_____
_____

1.9 **The young children speak politely.**
1. Is *children* the subject or the verb? _____
2. Which word is an adverb of manner? _____
3. Which word is an irregular plural noun? _____
4. Diagram the sentence here.

1.10 **Paris is a popular city.**
1. Is *Paris* a common noun or a proper noun? _____
2. What is the linking verb? _____
3. Which words does the linking verb link? _____
4. Diagram the sentence here.

1.11 **The old turtle moves slowly.**
1. Is *moves* the subject or the verb? _____
2. What part of speech is *slowly*? _____
3. Which word is an article? _____
4. Diagram the sentence here.

1.3 More Singular and Plural Nouns

Most plural nouns are formed by adding -s. Some plurals are formed by adding -es. Some plurals have spelling changes but do not add -s or -es. Other plurals do not change from their singular forms.

Write the plural form of each noun.

1. studio _____
2. potato _____
3. piano _____
4. woman _____
5. ox _____
6. species _____

7. stereo _____
8. hero _____
9. auto _____
10. child _____
11. mouse _____
12. corps _____

Circle the singular noun in each sentence. Then write the plural of the noun.

13. Did your friends send you that photo of us? _____

14. A sheep is grazing behind the two barns. _____

15. The man carried the paddles to the boats. _____

16. All the students stared at the prehistoric tooth. _____

17. The women chose the dress with the best colors. _____

18. This ripe tomato looks perfect for our tacos. _____

19. Your suitcase is too heavy. _____

20. The eggs of a goose are quite large. _____

Complete each sentence with plural of the noun or nouns in parentheses.

21. The gardeners had a problem with _____ (deer) eating the vegetables.

22. We laughed so hard when we watched the old _____ (movie).

23. My sister likes to wear _____ (scarf) during the winter.

24. He has a few _____ (radio) that are 20 years old.

25. If I don't brush my _____ (tooth), I could get _____ (cavity).

26. Several _____ (ox) and _____ (donkey) carried the heavy loads.

27. The thirteen _____ (colony) later became the first _____ (state).

28. We saw _____ (goose) and _____ (seagull) at the lake.

For additional help, review pages 6–7 in your textbook or visit www.voyagesinenglish.com.

Section 1 • 7

1.4 Possessive Nouns

The possessive form of a noun expresses possession, or ownership. The apostrophe (') is the sign of a **possessive noun.**

Write the singular and plural possessive form of each noun.

1. baby _____
2. man _____
3. deer _____
4. guppy _____
5. hero _____

6. cat _____
7. child _____
8. bear _____
9. Scott _____
10. woman _____

Underline the possessive noun in each sentence. Circle *S* if it is singular or *P* if it is plural.

11. Jesse's prize calf won the first place ribbon at the state fair. S P
12. The sheep's stalls are at the end of the livestock barn. S P
13. Most of the fair's events are held during the last three days. S P
14. One of my favorite places to visit is the children's petting zoo. S P
15. The horses' barn is where I hang out after the events are over. S P

Rewrite each of the following, using a possessive noun. Then write *singular* or *plural* to identify the possessive noun.

16. the fur of the bear _____ _____
17. the styles of the women _____ _____
18. the cheers of the people _____ _____
19. the song of the band _____ _____
20. the paintings of the children _____ _____
21. the report of Maria _____ _____
22. the homework of the students _____ _____
24. the plays of the classes _____ _____
25. the speeches of the teachers _____ _____

Write a sentence that uses both the singular and plural possessive forms of *man*.

26. _____

For additional help, review pages 8–9 in your textbook or visit www.voyagesinenglish.com.

1.5 Collective Nouns

A **collective noun** names a group of people, animals, places, or things that are considered a unit. A collective noun usually acts as a singular noun.

Write a collective noun for each word.

1. players _____
2. relatives _____
3. elk _____
4. people _____
5. turkeys _____

6. soldiers _____
7. musicians _____
8. actors _____
9. workers _____
10. teachers _____

Underline the collective noun or nouns in each sentence.

11. A flock of geese flies over the lake.

12. The speaker faced the audience and began her presentation.

13. A swarm of bees buzzed around the group of picnickers.

14. A soccer team in England is known as a football club.

15. The chorus walked onstage, and the quartet began to play.

16. Our school play had quite a cast of characters.

17. The school faculty agree to meet with the student council.

18. It is the jury who will decide whether the crew is guilty.

19. Whenever the band begins to play, a crowd gathers to watch.

Underline the collective noun in each sentence. Then circle the verb that correctly completes the sentence.

20. Our school basketball team (practice   practices) in a gymnasium.

21. Mr. Wilkins's science class (go   goes) on a field trip each year.

22. A bunch of purple grapes (sit   sits) in the yellow bowl.

23. The flock of sheep restlessly (waits   wait) for its meal.

24. That company of soldiers (receive   receives) new orders tonight.

25. A crew of workers (wait   waits) for supplies to arrive.

26. The Thomas family (takes   takes) a vacation every August.

27. This rowdy audience (applaud   applauds) enthusiastically after every solo.

For additional help, review pages 10–11 in your textbook or visit www.voyagesinenglish.com.

Section 1 • 9

1.6 Nouns as Subjects and Subject Complements

A noun can be the **subject** of a verb. The subject tells what a sentence is about. A noun can be a **subject complement.** A subject complement follows a linking verb and renames the subject.

Underline the subject once and the subject complement twice in each sentence.

1. Andy Davis is my brother.

2. My father is an inspiration to me.

3. She will always be an enthusiastic learner.

4. The strongest supporter of all the teams is Mr. Barrons.

5. Mrs. Pearson's son is a doctor at the hospital.

6. Glen Ellen High School was the location for this year's championship game.

7. Mr. Chu is a gym teacher at our school.

8. Abraham Lincoln was the 16th president of the United States.

9. His most famous speech is the Gettysburg Address.

10. Phillis Wheatley was an American poet.

11. Antietam was an important battle during the Civil War.

12. The Ornithopter was an aircraft designed by Leonardo da Vinci.

13. Several books were the prize for the winning essay.

14. Spinach is a vegetable that is high in iron and Vitamin A.

15. Each volunteer is a graduate of the community college.

For each word write two sentences. In the first sentence, use the word as a subject. In the second sentence, use the same word as a subject complement.

16. invitation _____

_____

17. assembly _____

_____

18. speech _____

_____

© Loyola Press. Voyages in English Grade 5

For additional help, review pages 12–13 in your textbook or visit www.voyagesinenglish.com.

1.7 Nouns as Objects

A noun can be used as a **direct object** of a verb. The direct object answers the question *whom* or *what* after an action verb. A noun can also be the **object of a preposition.** Prepositions show place, time, direction, and relationship.

Underline the direct object in each sentence.

1. Carlos Santana plays guitar.
2. The audience appreciates music.
3. Oscar always carries a calculator.
4. Jennifer plays violin.
5. Those children have entered many musical competitions.

Circle the preposition in each sentence. Then underline the object of the preposition.

6. A kazoo is played with the lips.
7. The hurdy-gurdy is a funny name for a musical instrument.
8. A drummer can make a crisp sound on a goblet drum.
9. The audience listens attentively to each melody.
10. A stringed instrument with a round back is a lute.

Complete each sentence with an object. Circle the number of each sentence where you added an object of a preposition.

11. I enjoy _reading_.
12. I jumped on the _trampoline_.
13. I wait by the _pool_.
14. I watch _tv._
15. I play after _school_.
16. I read _books_.
17. I have _a sister_.
18. I eat before _school_.
19. I draw _pictures_.
20. I rest under a _tree_.

Complete each sentence by writing a direct object and an object of a preposition.

21. Many people enjoy _pasta_
22. My sister and I purchased _a toy_
23. The neighbor next door took _my favorite toy._
24. I cleaned _my room_

For additional help, review pages 14–15 in your textbook or visit www.voyagesinenglish.com.

Section 1 • 11

1.7   Nouns as Objects

A noun can be used as a **direct object** of a verb. The direct object answers the question *whom* or *what* after an action verb. A noun can also be the **object of a preposition.** Prepositions show place, time, direction, and relationship.

Circle the verb and underline the direct object in each sentence. Write whether the direct object tells *whom* or *what*.

1. A cartoonist draws cartoons.   _____

2. These cartoons show people in funny situations.   _____

3. A cartoonist first sketches pictures with a pencil.   _____

4. I drew my best friend as a cartoon character.   _____

5. Both magazines and newspapers print cartoons.   _____

Circle the preposition in each sentence. Then underline the object of the preposition.

6. Artists throughout the world use clay.

7. Admirers of this local artist collect his work.

8. My art teacher has studied art for many years.

9. These paintings on the wall were completed recently.

10. I would really like a portrait of my new puppy.

Complete each sentence by writing a direct object and an object of a preposition.

11. Brent practices _____ with the school _____.

12. Our team won a _____ in the _____.

13. I wrote a _____ after _____.

14. The coach of my _____ demonstrated _____.

15. Children around our _____ often play _____.

16. A group of _____ hiked the _____ yesterday.

Write three sentences about things you enjoy doing and when or where you do them. Underline each direct object and circle each object of a preposition.

17. _____

18. _____

19. _____

© Loyola Press. Voyages in English   Grade 5

For additional help, review pages 14–15 in your textbook or visit www.voyagesinenglish.com.

1.8 Nouns as Indirect Objects

A noun can be the **indirect object** of a verb. The indirect object tells *to whom*, *to what*, *for whom*, or *for what* the action was done. A sentence can have an indirect object only if it has a direct object.

Circle the indirect object in each sentence. The direct object is italicized.

1. Mrs. Swain bought Shana a new *dress* for the party.

2. Mr. Chin showed the class his *pictures* of Africa.

3. Dad gave Tad *permission* to use the car.

4. Our community center offers homeless people *shelter*.

5. The child care program brought the center statewide *attention*.

6. A skateboard team promised the afterschool club a *demonstration*.

7. Robert and his friends offer young kids tennis *lessons*.

8. Mr. Williams teaches them basic *skills* in math.

9. Briana handed the children important safety *equipment*.

10. The president awarded the crew a *medal* of honor.

Underline the direct object and circle the indirect object in each sentence.

11. Manuel sold his cousin a used computer.

12. The mayor promised our town a new library.

13. Ms. Howe gave the groups time for their projects.

14. I always tell my friends jokes.

15. The mail carrier brought Lisa a package.

16. The food pantry gives local families groceries.

Rewrite each sentence so that it has an indirect object.

17. Ms. Thomas assigned a research project to our class.

_____

18. His younger brother paid too much money to the clerk.

_____

19. The magician showed a fascinating card trick to the audience.

_____

For additional help, review pages 16–17 in your textbook
or visit www.voyagesinenglish.com.

Section 1 • 13

1.8 Nouns as Indirect Objects

A noun can be the **indirect object** of a verb. The indirect object tells *to whom*, *to what*, *for whom*, or *for what* the action was done. A sentence can have an indirect object only if it has a direct object.

Underline the direct object and circle the indirect object in each sentence.

1. Dad promised our family a camping trip at the lake up north.
2. Dad built Ben a wooden canoe of his own.
3. Ms. Cahill gave Ben maps of the wilderness areas in Canada.
4. Ben showed his friends the places he wanted to go.
5. Just before they left, Ben gave his sister a toy paddle.

Write an indirect object that completes each sentence.

6. The firefighters told _____ the plan for evacuating the school.
7. Many students promised the _____ an orderly exit.
8. The school administration gave _____ a practice fire alarm exercise.
9. The teachers taught _____ the exit route.
10. I offered _____ tutoring help after school.
11. The principal awarded _____ the Helpful Tutor prize this week.
12. Jody reads _____ silly poems and funny stories.
13. Many volunteers give _____ their time and devotion.
14. Volunteers everywhere offer _____ hope and support.
15. Some of those same people now lend _____ their time and help.

Complete each sentence by writing an indirect object and a direct object.

16. The city council promised _____.
17. The coach of the soccer team showed _____.
18. The team manager handed _____.
19. Paul offered _____.
20. To start the game, the center kicked _____.
21. The referee blew his whistle and gave _____.

For additional help, review pages 16–17 in your textbook or visit www.voyagesinenglish.com.

1.11 Words Used as Nouns or as Adjectives

A noun names a person, place, or thing. An adjective describes a noun. Many words can be used as either nouns or adjectives.

Write whether each underlined word is a noun or an adjective.

1. Did you know there are 30 <u>professional</u> teams in this league? _____

2. Using <u>public</u> transportation helps cut down on air pollution. _____

3. The flowers blooming in the <u>garden</u> are beautiful. _____

4. The gift our class gave to Mr. Henderson was a <u>surprise</u> to him. _____

5. The <u>debate</u> team has a big competition in two weeks. _____

Use each word in the box to complete two of the sentences. For each sentence write *noun* **or** *adjective* **to identify how the word is used.**

football	ocean	mountain	magazine

6. Huge _____ waves crashed on the sandy shore. _____

7. This _____ contains several interesting articles. _____

8. The high school _____ game went into overtime. _____

9. The Sierras are a _____ range in California. _____

10. We stood on the peak of the _____. _____

11. He caught the _____ and ran down the field. _____

12. I read a _____ article about coin collecting. _____

13. She gazed at the blue _____ before her. _____

Write two sentences for each word. Use it once as a noun and once as an adjective.

14. apple _____

_____

15. history _____

_____

16. gold _____

_____

For additional help, review pages 22–23 in your textbook or visit www.voyagesinenglish.com.

Section 1 • 17

SECTION 2 | Daily Maintenance

2.1 **Brandon has an older brother.**
1. Which word is a common noun?   _____
2. Which word is a proper noun?   _____
3. What is the subject?   _____
4. Diagram the sentence here.

2.2 **The choir performed three songs.**
1. Is the verb regular or irregular?   _____
2. What part of speech is *three*?   _____
3. Which word is a collective noun?   _____
4. Diagram the sentence here.

2.3 **The shy girl speaks quietly.**
1. What part of speech is *quietly*?   _____
2. Which word is an article?   _____
3. Is the noun singular or plural?   _____
4. Diagram the sentence here.

2.4 **I enjoyed Rick's funny story.**
1. Is *I* a subject pronoun or an object pronoun? _____
2. Which word is a possessive noun?   _____
3. Which word is an adjective?   _____
4. Diagram the sentence here.

2.5 **The bunnies' tails are brown.**
1. What is the simple subject?
2. What is the subject complement?
3. Is the possessive noun singular or plural?
4. Diagram the sentence here.

_____
_____
_____

2.6 **Robert Frost was a famous poet.**
1. What is the subject?
2. What is the subject complement?
3. Is *was* a linking verb or an action verb?
4. Diagram the sentence here.

_____
_____
_____

2.7 **We neatly folded the clean clothes.**
1. Is the verb present tense or past tense?
2. Which word is a direct object?
3. Which word is an adverb?
4. Diagram the sentence here.

_____
_____
_____

2.8 **Mr. Ramos promised the workers a raise.**
1. Is the verb regular or irregular?
2. Which word is a direct object?
3. Which word is an indirect object?
4. Diagram the sentence here.

_____
_____
_____

Grade 5

2.9 **The children played a game.**
1. What is the verb?   _____
2. Which word is an irregular plural noun?   _____
3. Is the verb present tense or past tense?   _____
4. Diagram the sentence here.

2.10 **Sean may attend the dance.**
1. Which word is an article?   _____
2. Which word is a helping verb?   _____
3. Is *dance* used as a noun or as a verb?   _____
4. Diagram the sentence here.

2.11 **He never misses baseball practice.**
1. What part of speech is *He*?   _____
2. Is the subject singular or plural?   _____
3. Is *baseball* used as a noun or as an adjective?   _____
4. Diagram the sentence here.

2.3 Subject Pronouns

A **subject pronoun** tells who or what the sentence is about. The subject pronouns are *I, you, he, she, it, we,* and *they.* A subject pronoun can also take the place of a noun used as a subject complement.

Underline the pronoun used as a subject in each sentence.

1. He wrote about Santorini, a famous volcano in Greece.

2. It last erupted in 1950.

3. They named it in the 13th century after Saint Irene.

4. I read that the volcano exploded and formed many islands.

5. You should see the photos my friend took while in Greece.

6. Some day we would like to plan a trip there.

7. Do you think Mr. Wilson would let us find out more about this location?

8. Usually, he encourages us to investigate new places.

Circle the pronoun in each sentence. Then circle whether the pronoun is used as a subject (S) or a subject complement (SC).

9. We saw a movie that shows the eruption of a volcano.   S   SC

10. The spectators in the first row were they.   S   SC

11. The photographer at the scene was he.   S   SC

12. You wouldn't believe all the smoke and ash in the air.   S   SC

13. The witnesses to the eruption were they.   S   SC

14. She talked about the rumbling sound of the volcano.   S   SC

15. It belched out rivers of steaming, molten lava.   S   SC

16. He interviewed other witnesses.   S   SC

17. The most frightened witness was she.   S   SC

18. We told our friends about this fascinating movie.   S   SC

Write two sentences using pronouns. Use the pronoun as the subject in the first sentence and as a subject complement in the second sentence.

19. _____

20. _____

For additional help, review pages 32–33 in your textbook or visit www.voyagesinenglish.com.

2.4 Object Pronouns

An **object pronoun** is a personal pronoun that is used as the object of a verb. A **direct object** names the receiver of the action of the verb. An **object of a preposition** follows a preposition.

Underline the pronoun used as a direct object in each sentence.

1. Zeus was the king of the gods, and many worshipped him long ago.

2. Hera married him, and together they had many children.

3. Zeus warned them about his sacred bird, the golden eagle.

4. Zeus's exploits and accomplishments astound us.

5. These fascinating stories interest me.

Underline the pronoun used as an object of a preposition in each sentence.

6. After reading a Greek myth, I imagine I have a part in it.

7. I climb the rocks and squeeze between them as if I'm Hercules.

8. The wind is the voice of a goddess, and I listen to her.

9. Her howling and whistling voice flows over me.

10. The clouds gather, and I imagine the gods' anger directed at us.

Underline the pronoun in each sentence. Then circle whether the pronoun is used as a direct object (*DO*) or as the object of a preposition (*OP*).

11. Ron entertained me with the movie *Jason and the Argonauts*.   DO   OP

12. I go to the movies with him every weekend.   DO   OP

13. Jason searches for the golden fleece, and the gods help him.   DO   OP

14. Jason assembled a crew, and Hercules sailed with them.   DO   OP

15. Did Ron ever thank you for the movie tickets?   DO   OP

16. Skeleton armies, snakes, and giants fight him in the exciting plot.   DO   OP

17. Poseidon sets the sea against them to block the route.   DO   OP

18. The crew could have easily been beaten by them.   DO   OP

19. Hera, queen of the gods, protected him and the crew.   DO   OP

20. The special effects in the movie intrigued us.   DO   OP

21. Ron said he will watch the DVD with me again.   DO   OP

For additional help, review pages 34–35 in your textbook or visit www.voyagesinenglish.com.

2.4 Object Pronouns

An **object pronoun** is a personal pronoun that is used as the object of a verb. A **direct object** names the receiver of the action of the verb. An **object of a preposition** follows a preposition.

Circle whether the underlined word in each sentence is a subject pronoun (*SP*) or an object pronoun (*OP*).

1. <u>He</u> dreamed he was alone on a deserted island.   SP OP
2. Water completely surrounded <u>him</u>.   SP OP
3. The only person standing on the beach was <u>he</u>.   SP OP
4. Do <u>you</u> know what it feels like to be truly alone?   SP OP
5. <u>It</u> can be a very eerie feeling.   SP OP
6. An island is filled with living things, even if you can't see <u>them</u>. SP OP
7. Long ago my sister read the book *Swiss Family Robinson* to <u>me</u>. SP OP
8. <u>She</u> gave the impression that living on an island would be fun.   SP OP
9. The story tells about a shipwrecked family and what happened to <u>them</u>. SP OP
10. <u>They</u> weren't alone because pirates also roamed the island.   SP OP
11. Do <u>you</u> think it is worse to be alone or to be surrounded by pirates? SP OP
12. This adventure story captivated <u>us</u>.   SP OP

Write an object pronoun that completes each sentence. Then write whether the pronoun is a direct object (*DO*) or an object of a preposition (*OP*).

13. Odysseus was a king, and a brave crew sailed with _____.   _____
14. A wooden horse helped _____ get inside the Trojan city.   _____
15. This event ended the 10-year war between the Greeks and _____. _____
16. The story of the Trojan horse was told to _____ in history class. _____
17. My younger sister likes the version of the story told by _____. _____

Write a sentence using each pair of pronouns.

18. he, them _____
19. you, us _____
20. it, her _____
21. we, him _____

For additional help, review pages 34–35 in your textbook or visit www.voyagesinenglish.com.

2.5 Indirect Objects

Pronouns can be the indirect object in a sentence. The **indirect object** tells *to whom*, *for whom*, *to what*, or *for what* the action is done. Object pronouns are used as indirect objects: *me, us, you, him, her, it,* and *them.*

Underline the personal pronoun used as an indirect object in each sentence. The direct object is italicized.

1. Books tell us different *stories* about a variety of topics.

2. I gave her a *copy* of my favorite book.

3. My teacher showed me a *list* of titles that have won awards.

4. The list showed us different *categories* for themes, artwork, and interest levels.

5. The children's section of a public library offers them a *choice* of free books.

6. Maya sent him several *books* she finished over the summer.

7. In return he made her the most thoughtful thank-you *card.*

8. Maya and the library have lent us a huge *supply* of books for the upcoming year.

Rewrite each sentence, replacing the italicized words with a pronoun.

9. Mrs. Owens gave *each student in the class* a library card.

   _____

10. Several children brought *the library staff* old books to sell.

    _____

11. Mom and Dad granted *Lisa and me* permission to donate some of our books.

    _____

12. We offered *Kate and Sam* our assistance.

    _____

13. I promised *Mr. Tien* an extra-credit assignment by reporting on the event.

    _____

14. The volunteers showed *the customers* the price list for the used books.

    _____

15. The principal presented *our class* with an award for our efforts that day.

    _____

For additional help, review pages 36–37 in your textbook or visit www.voyagesinenglish.com.

2.6 Uses of Pronouns

Pronouns are used in different ways in sentences. The subject pronouns are *I, you, he, she, it, we,* and *they.* The object pronouns are *me, you, him, her, it, us,* and *them.*

Underline each subject pronoun once and each object pronoun twice.

1. She drove us to the museum.

2. Will you read me the story about Achilles on the plaque above the mural?

3. I think this story about him is fascinating.

4. The main character of *The Iliad* was he, who gave us an account of the Trojan War.

5. He fought with them until his withdrawal from battle.

6. They told us the term "Achilles' heel" came from how Achilles died.

7. My friend and I enjoyed sharing the exhibits with them.

Circle the pronoun that correctly completes each sentence.

8. Chan and (me   I) are trying out for the academic team this year.

9. Will you lend (me   I) your book on Greek mythology?

10. That copy of *Ancient Greek Philosophy* belongs to (they   them).

11. I told (she   her) about my plan.

12. Our team instructor is (her   she).

13. (Them   They) are knowledgeable players.

14. Some people saw (I   me) in the library.

15. Tell (them   they) about the academic team tryouts.

16. Does this book belong to (him   he)?

17. (Him   He) will be an incredible asset to our team.

18. We clapped for (him   he) when his name was announced.

19. The students already chosen for the academic team are (they   them).

Write two sentences about a good friend. Use subject pronouns and object pronouns in your sentences.

20. _____

21. _____

For additional help, review pages 38–39 in your textbook or visit www.voyagesinenglish.com.

Section 2 • 27

2.7 | Possessive Pronouns and Adjectives

A **possessive pronoun** shows possession or ownership and takes the place of a possessive noun. A **possessive adjective** also shows possession, but it is always used before a noun.

Underline the possessive pronoun in each sentence.

1. Rafael, these markers are yours.

2. The task of coaching students was his.

3. Hers is the folder with little yellow flowers.

4. Ours are the black and white checkered ones.

5. These new bicycles are theirs.

6. This set of art supplies is mine.

7. His is the backpack covered with animal stickers.

Circle the possessive adjective in each sentence.

8. My favorite story is about Atlas carrying the world.

9. Carrying the weight of the world was his punishment.

10. Her report included illustrations, maps, and photos.

11. The ability to give a concise and factual presentation was her advantage.

12. What is the topic of your presentation?

13. Your eyes look tired after all the reading you have done.

14. Their efforts will not go unnoticed or unrewarded.

Write a possessive pronoun or a possessive adjective to complete each sentence.

15. The students displayed _____ presentations along the classroom wall.

16. _____ included a photo he took on a visit to Athens.

17. The Parthenon, with _____ many columns, is an example of Greek architecture.

18. _____ map of the archipelago was drawn well.

19. _____ presentation, which I finished last night, included this model.

20. The building of the Trojan horse was the topic of _____ report.

21. Alicia, did you choose Athens as the topic of _____?

22. It is _____ job to make sure I learn new things.

For additional help, review pages 40–41 in your textbook or visit www.voyagesinenglish.com.

2.8 Intensive and Reflexive Pronouns

Intensive and reflexive pronouns end in *self* or *selves*. An intensive pronoun is used to emphasize a noun that comes before it. A reflexive pronoun is used as the direct or indirect object of a verb or as the object of a preposition.

Underline the intensive or reflexive pronoun in each sentence. Circle the word to which the pronoun refers.

1. The students themselves raised money for a trip to the natural history museum.

2. We gave ourselves two weekends to plan for the yard sale.

3. I myself brought toys, old skateboards, and sports gear.

4. The principal herself donated books and DVDs.

5. You can see for yourself all the different items we have for sale.

6. He built himself a table for all his electronic gear.

7. We really wanted to pay for the museum trip ourselves.

Underline the intensive or reflexive pronoun in each sentence. Circle whether each pronoun is singular (*S*) or plural (*P*).

8. I made myself a map of the Aegean Sea.   S   P

9. It includes many islands, and they themselves made it a difficult project.   S   P

10. Sophia handed out copies of my map to herself and the class.   S   P

11. I think the map itself is a work of art.   S   P

12. The class could see copies of the ancient maps in the library themselves.   S   P

Write a sentence for each word, using it as either an intensive or a reflexive pronoun.

13. myself _____

14. yourselves _____

15. herself _____

16. itself _____

17. ourselves _____

18. himself _____

19. yourself _____

20. themselves _____

For additional help, review pages 42–43 in your textbook or visit www.voyagesinenglish.com.

2.9 Antecedents

The word to which a pronoun refers is its **antecedent.** The antecedent is the word that the pronoun replaces. The pronoun must agree with its antecedent in person and number and in whether it refers to a male, a female, or a thing.

Underline the pronoun in each sentence. Circle the pronoun's antecedent.

1. Birds have a place in mythology because they are seen as pure and wise.

2. The phoenix is a mythical firebird; it is part of Greek mythology.

3. The Greeks imagined the bird like a peacock, and they claimed it lived in Phoenicia.

4. Chinese mythology has an important bird; it is also called the phoenix.

5. The goddess Venus preferred the dove; she considered this bird a symbol of love.

6. When our leaders chose a national symbol, they wanted a noble bird.

7. Ben Franklin suggested the turkey; he claimed turkeys were brave.

8. Others wanted the bald eagle because it was a symbol of strength and freedom.

Write a sentence to answer each question. Use a pronoun to replace the italicized antecedent or antecedents.

9. Did *Toby* show up for the play rehearsal?

_____

10. Is the *play* a comedy or a tragedy?

_____

11. Is *Tania* going to play the lead role?

_____

12. Will there be room in the cast for *Dylan and Mark*?

_____

13. If Toby plays Zeus, what role will *David* play?

_____

14. Do you think the *music* will be live or recorded?

_____

15. When will the *art class* have the *sets* ready?

_____

For additional help, review pages 44–45 in your textbook or visit www.voyagesinenglish.com.

2.11 Demonstrative and Interrogative Pronouns

Demonstrative pronouns are used to point out people, places, and things. An **interrogative pronoun** is used to ask a question.

Write a demonstrative pronoun to complete each sentence. Follow the directions in parentheses.

1. _____ are good references for the report. (plural, near)

2. Is _____ a statue of Thomas Jefferson? (singular, far)

3. _____ are the students I was telling you about. (plural, far)

4. _____ are fantastic! (plural, near)

5. _____ is the landmark I refer to in my report. (singular, near)

6. Will _____ take me very long to research? (singular, far)

Circle the interrogative pronoun that correctly completes each sentence.

7. (Whom   Who) saw the shooting stars last night?

8. (What   Whose) have you seen through your telescope?

9. (Whom   Who) does Mia prefer to help?

10. (Whose   What) was the latest report on the traffic?

11. (Who   Whom) is Ms. Sutton's assistant?

12. (What   Who) happened after the game?

13. (Who   Whose) is the backpack with the red stripe?

Write a question that uses each pair of pronouns correctly.

14. what, those

_____

15. who, this

_____

16. whom, these

_____

17. what, that

_____

18. who, these

_____

For additional help, review pages 48–49 in your textbook or visit www.voyagesinenglish.com.

Section 2 • 33

SECTION 3 | Daily Maintenance

3.1 **I handed the librarian the overdue books.**
1. Which noun is the direct object? _____
2. Which noun is the indirect object _____
3. Which word is a personal pronoun? _____
4. Diagram the sentence here.

3.2 **The teacher showed us a world map.**
1. What is the complete subject? _____
2. Is the pronoun singular or plural? _____
3. What is the object pronoun? _____
4. Diagram the sentence here.

3.3 **They gave me a blue bicycle.**
1. Which word is a subject pronoun? _____
2. Which word is the indirect object? _____
3. What part of speech is *blue*? _____
4. Diagram the sentence here.

3.4 **Ava and I are best friends.**
1. Is the subject or the predicate compound? _____
2. What is the subject complement? _____
3. Is *are* used as a linking verb or a helping verb? _____
4. Diagram the sentence here.

© Loyola Press. Voyages in English Grade 5

3.5 **The dog's owner is she.**
1. How is *she* used in the sentence?   _____
2. Which noun does *she* rename?   _____
3. Is the possessive noun singular or plural?   _____
4. Diagram the sentence here.

3.6 **This red backpack is his.**
1. Which word is a demonstrative adjective?   _____
2. Which word is a possessive pronoun?   _____
3. Which word is a linking verb?   _____
4. Diagram the sentence here.

3.7 **We are rehearsing our presentation.**
1. What is the verb phrase?   _____
2. Which word is a possessive adjective?   _____
3. What word is a plural personal pronoun?   _____
4. Diagram the sentence here.

3.8 **The company will send me the product.**
1. What is the verb phrase?   _____
2. What tense is the verb phrase?   _____
3. What is the object pronoun?   _____
4. Diagram the sentence here.

3.9 **He is Ryan's younger brother.**
1. Which word does *brother* rename?   _____
2. Which word is a comparative adjective?   _____
3. Is the possessive noun singular or plural?   _____
4. Diagram the sentence here.

3.10 **Who sent you the package?**
1. What part of speech is the indirect object?   _____
2. Which word is an interrogative pronoun?   _____
3. Is the article definite or indefinite?   _____
4. Diagram the sentence here.

3.11 **That is the city's tallest building.**
1. What kind of noun is *city's*?   _____
2. Which word is a demonstrative pronoun?   _____
3. What kind of adjective is *tallest*?   _____
4. Diagram the sentence here.

3.1 Descriptive Adjectives

Descriptive adjectives tell about the size, shape, color, or weight of the nouns they describe. They can tell how something looks, sounds, tastes, smells, or feels. A descriptive adjective generally comes before a noun.

Underline the descriptive adjective or adjectives in each sentence. Circle the noun each adjective describes.

1. A paleontologist studies prehistoric life on Earth.

2. Dinosaurs roamed during that time and were the dominant species.

3. Big dinosaurs with long necks mostly ate vegetation.

4. They had small heads and short legs.

5. Birds have a close relationship with dinosaurs.

6. A prehistoric fossil of a bird was found in Germany in 1861.

7. The *Archaeopteryx* has similar features as those of the theropod dinosaur.

8. Unlike modern birds, it had small teeth and a long, bony tail.

9. The fossil shows critical evidence that birds may have evolved from dinosaurs.

10. Fossils provide important information about the past.

Write a descriptive adjective before each noun.

11.	_____ background	16.	_____ research
12.	_____ work	17.	_____ care
13.	_____ process	18.	_____ box
14.	_____ gloves	19.	_____ shirt
15.	_____ hat	20.	_____ job

Complete each sentence with an appropriate descriptive adjective.

21. One _____ day the winds never seemed to end.

22. Sand was blowing over the _____ fossils we had unearthed.

23. All we could do was cover them with _____ tarps.

24. Our _____ tents held up against the sandstorm.

25. Such _____ storms can last for days.

26. At last the _____ winds stopped, and we could return to work.

For additional help, review pages 54–55 in your textbook or visit www.voyagesinenglish.com.

3.2 Proper Adjectives

Some descriptive adjectives come from proper nouns and are called **proper adjectives.** Like proper nouns, proper adjectives begin with capital letters.

Write the proper adjective for each proper noun.

1. America _____
2. Africa _____
3. Texas _____
4. Germany _____
5. China _____

6. Alaska _____
7. Rome _____
8. Ireland _____
9. Spain _____
10. Wales _____

Write a proper adjective for each proper noun. Then write a sentence using the adjective correctly.

11. Switzerland _____

_____

12. Britain _____

_____

13. Canada _____

_____

14. Shakespeare _____

_____

15. Greece _____

_____

Use the noun in parentheses to write a proper adjective that completes each sentence.

16. An _____ scientist discovered the *Apatosaurus* in 1879. (America)
17. A _____ fossil hunter named the *Megalosaurus*. (Britain)
18. This rich fossil site is in the _____ Islands. (Hawaii)
19. A _____ study was done on fossil fish. (Sweden)
20. Have _____ scientists been involved in these studies? (France)

© Loyola Press. Voyages in English **Grade 5**

For additional help, review pages 56–57 in your textbook or visit www.voyagesinenglish.com.

3.3 | Articles

A, an, and *the* are **articles.** *A* and *an* are indefinite articles that refer to any one of a class of things. *The* is the definite article. It refers to one or more specific people, places, or things.

Write the correct indefinite article, *a* or *an*, before each item.

1. _____ dinosaur

2. _____ insect

3. _____ bird

4. _____ *Tyrannosaurus rex*

5. _____ octagon

6. _____ alligator

7. _____ ancient fossil

8. _____ shovel

9. _____ invention

10. _____ rock sample

11. _____ incredible discovery

12. _____ paleontologist

Circle the indefinite articles and underline the definite articles in these sentences.

13. A Petoskey stone is made of fossilized coral.

14. It can be found along the shoreline of northern Michigan.

15. My brother found a rock that had fossils of shells embedded in it.

16. The rock also had an impression of a worm.

17. It is fun to imagine living in the time of prehistoric animals.

18. We used to explore the caves near our old house.

19. It was there that I found a fossil of a fish.

20. My dad called the college, and a professor came to inspect the fossil.

Complete each sentence. Use at least one article.

21. In prehistoric times, _____.

22. Plant-eating dinosaurs had _____ and _____.

23. Fossils are _____.

24. Paleontology is _____.

25. One theory why the dinosaurs vanished is that _____.

26. The disappearance of the dinosaurs will _____.

27. The discovery of ancient fossils is _____.

28. Would you want to _____?

For additional help, review pages 58–59 in your textbook or visit www.voyagesinenglish.com.

Section 3 • 39

3.4 Repetition of Articles

When two or more nouns joined by *and* refer to different people, places, or things, use an article before each noun. This **repetition of articles** shows that the two nouns are different.

Circle whether each underlined phrase refers to one (*1*) or more than one (*>1*) person, place, or thing.

1. <u>A scientist and a student</u> worked to uncover the bones.   1   >1
2. <u>A paleontologist and artist</u> drew how the dinosaur may have looked.   1   >1
3. <u>The professor and a writer</u> wrote the history of the dinosaur.   1   >1
4. <u>The student of paleontology and editor</u> reviewed the article.   1   >1
5. The article was read by <u>the science club and the college students</u>.   1   >1

Write an article where one is needed. Write X if no article is needed.

6. There was one presenter: _____ professor and _____ discoverer of the site.

7. Two students helped: _____ assistant and _____ copyeditor.

8. One scientist verified the data: _____ paleontologist and _____ researcher.

9. The next presenter was _____ music student from Mrs. Gray's class.

10. During the concert two people played: _____ piano teacher and _____ violinist.

Write a sentence for each set of words, using repetition of articles as needed.

11. Louis, friend and science partner

_____

12. two people: one is a writer and the other is a poet

_____

13. one person: sculptor and painter

_____

14. Jennifer, lab assistant and student

_____

15. two people: a doctor and a scientist

_____

© Loyola Press. Voyages in English **Grade 5**

For additional help, review pages 60–61 in your textbook or visit www.voyagesinenglish.com.

3.7 Adjectives as Subject Complements

An adjective that follows a linking verb and completes the sentence is called a **subject complement.** The subject complement describes the subject of the sentence.

Circle the subject complement in each sentence. Underline the noun the subject complement describes.

1. The shipwreck was deep under the water.

2. This ship was large and once carried valuable cargo.

3. The two storms were severe and endangered many ships.

4. Many artifacts carried by the ship were rare.

5. Each crate was massive and held several valuable objects.

6. The recovery crew became excited when they found the ship.

7. A recovery submarine is remote-controlled by someone on a ship.

8. These cameras are powerful and show details of the wreck.

Underline the adjective in each sentence. Circle whether the adjective is a subject complement (*SC*) or comes before the noun (*BN*).

9. Paleontologists find buried fossils throughout the world.   SC   BN

10. Los Angeles has a special site filled with fossils.   SC   BN

11. The La Brea Tar Pits in the city are spectacular.   SC   BN

12. This bone from a mastodon was huge.   SC   BN

13. Mammal fossils have been found in the pit.   SC   BN

14. I think the mastodons are amazing.   SC   BN

Write an adjective or adjectives to complete each sentence.

15. The exhibit at the zoo last week was _____.

16. The reptiles in the exhibit were _____.

17. A lizard's skin feels _____.

18. The skin of many reptiles is _____ and _____.

19. These _____ reptiles often move slowly.

20. Many students were _____ and _____ around the reptiles.

21. One _____ student even held a _____ snake.

For additional help, review pages 66–67 in your textbook or visit www.voyagesinenglish.com.

3.8 Adjectives That Compare

The **positive degree** of an adjective shows a quality of a noun. The **comparative degree** is used to compare two items or two sets of items. The **superlative degree** is used to compare three or more items.

Complete the chart.

POSITIVE	COMPARATIVE	SUPERLATIVE
1. light	_____	_____
2. cold	_____	_____
3. safe	_____	_____
4. big	_____	_____
5. pretty	_____	_____
6. good	_____	_____
7. bad	_____	_____

Circle the adjective that correctly completes each sentence. Then circle whether the degree of each adjective is positive (P), comparative (C), or superlative (S).

8. The (bigger   biggest) roller coaster I've ever seen is the Rattler.   P   C   S

9. This ride was especially (scary   scariest) for me.   P   C   S

10. I have been on (longer   longest) rides than this.   P   C   S

11. This trip was one of my (happy   happiest) memories.   P   C   S

12. Their (new   newest) ride of all always has very long lines.   P   C   S

13. The day seemed (long   longest), and I was tired when we left.   P   C   S

Complete each sentence. Include the comparative or superlative form of the italicized adjective.

14. My brother has *strong* arms, but _____.

15. The *small* boxes were easy to lift, but not as easy as _____.

16. Most loads are *heavy*, yet we are saving _____.

17. Our truck was *slow*, but then we passed _____.

18. I was *happy* to finish my work, but I was _____.

19. It would be *bad* if we were late, but _____.

20. Using small boxes was a *good* idea, but _____.

For additional help, review pages 68–69 in your textbook or visit www.voyagesinenglish.com.

3.9 *More, Most* and *Less, Least*

> Some adjectives do not add *-er* or *-est* to form the comparative and superlative degrees. The comparative is formed by adding *more* or *less* before the positive form of the adjective. The superlative is formed by adding *most* or *least*.

Use *more* and *most* to write the comparative and superlative degrees for each positive degree adjective.

1. important _____   _____

2. interesting _____   _____

3. generous _____   _____

4. adventurous _____   _____

5. enormous _____   _____

Use *less* and *least* to write the comparative and superlative degrees for each positive degree adjective.

6. bizarre _____   _____

7. successful _____   _____

8. delicious _____   _____

9. cautious _____   _____

10. aware _____   _____

Circle the word that correctly completes each sentence.

11. The trip to the craft fair was (least   less) interesting than the museum.

12. The hike to the mountain peak was my (more   most) adventurous trip ever.

13. I can't tell which is (more   most) intelligent, my dog or my cat.

14. I chose this rock hammer because it was the (least   less) expensive one.

15. It's the (more   most) important tool in my rock-collecting kit.

Write a sentence for each adjective, using the degree in parentheses.

16. powerful (comparative)

_____

17. fortunate (superlative)

_____

For additional help, review pages 70–71 in your textbook
or visit www.voyagesinenglish.com.

Section 3 • 45

3.10 *Fewer, Fewest* and *Less, Least*

Use *fewer* and *fewest* with concrete nouns that name things that you can see, touch, and count. Use *less* and *least* with abstract nouns that name things that generally cannot be seen, touched, or counted.

Cross out the phrase in each line that is written incorrectly.

1. fewer sunflowers   least rocks   fewest tools

2. less rain   few clouds   fewer wind

3. least amount   fewer snow   less water

4. fewest trees   least sun   fewer moisture

5. less plants   least food   fewer mountains

Circle the word that correctly completes each sentence.

6. After the tsunami there were (fewer   less) homes in the village.

7. There was (less   fewer) wind now than earlier in the day.

8. Water washed out the road, resulting in the transport of (fewer   least) supplies.

9. The (least   fewest) amount of damage was further up the mountain.

10. Along the shoreline is where the (fewest   least) animals were found.

Write a sentence for each word, using *less* or *fewer* to describe the noun.

11. footprints _____

12. food _____

13. interest _____

14. bones _____

15. books _____

Write a sentence for each word, using *least* or *fewest* to describe the noun.

16. boats _____

17. sunshine _____

18. turtles _____

19. time _____

20. knowledge _____

21. backpacks _____

For additional help, review pages 72–73 in your textbook or visit www.voyagesinenglish.com.

4.5 **This dance class has fewer students.**
1. Is *dance* used as a noun or an adjective?   _____
2. Which word is a collective noun?   _____
3. What is the comparative adjective?   _____
4. Diagram the sentence here.

4.6 **Three small kittens chased the blue string.**
1. What is the plural noun?   _____
2. Is the verb present tense or past tense?   _____
3. Which words are adjectives?   _____
4. Diagram the sentence here.

4.7 **The fastest runner won the race.**
1. Is the past tense verb regular or irregular?   _____
2. What are the nouns?   _____
3. Which word is a superlative adjective?   _____
4. Diagram the sentence here.

4.8 **Hers is the black sweater.**
1. Is *Hers* a pronoun or an adjective?   _____
2. What is the verb?   _____
3. Is the article definite or indefinite?   _____
4. Diagram the sentence here.

4.9 **Our new principal is friendly.**
1. What is the simple subject?   _____
2. Is *Our* a pronoun or an adjective?   _____
3. What is the subject complement?   _____
4. Diagram the sentence here.

4.10 **My parents gave me this necklace.**
1. What is the verb?   _____
2. Is *me* a subject pronoun or an object pronoun?   _____
3. Which word is a demonstrative adjective?   _____
4. Diagram the sentence here.

4.11 **Which car is less expensive?**
1. Is this sentence a statement or a question?   _____
2. Which words form a comparative adjective?   _____
3. Which word is an interrogative adjective?   _____
4. Diagram the sentence here.

4.1 Action Verbs and Being Verbs

A **verb** is a word used to express action or being. An action verb expresses action. A being verb expresses a state of being. The verb *be* and its various forms are the most common being verbs.

Underline the action verb in each sentence.

1. The bells in the clock tower chime every hour.

2. A mother walks her baby on the sidewalk.

3. I read an article about the new park.

4. Two teenagers skate through the park.

5. A school's track team runs by me.

6. Jennifer and Erin skip along the sidewalk.

7. A group of men laughed at a humorous story.

Circle the being verb in each sentence.

8. The weather was good the day of the race.

9. I was nervous at first.

10. Oatmeal is my favorite meal before a race.

11. Samuel, Robert, and Stephen were three of the athletes.

12. My family is proud of my participation.

13. The 100-yard dash and the 400-yard relay race are my events.

14. Both my mom and dad were track stars in high school.

Underline the verb in each sentence. Write whether the verb is an *action* verb or a *being* verb.

15. I enjoy strawberries on my cereal.   _____

16. Her favorite yogurt is strawberry-banana.   _____

17. Alicia sliced some kiwi fruit.   _____

18. Chopped almonds are another nice addition to yogurt. _____

19. Everyone gobbled this delicious breakfast.   _____

20. Terryl washed the dishes afterward.   _____

21. The twins stacked the clean bowls carefully on the shelf. _____

22. This meal was a good way to start the day.   _____

For additional help, review pages 80–81 in your textbook
or visit www.voyagesinenglish.com.

4.2 Verb Phrases

A **verb phrase** is a group of words that does the work of a single verb. A verb phrase contains a main verb and one or more **helping verbs.** In questions and some statements, the parts of the verb phrase may be separated.

Underline the verb phrase in each sentence.

1. After school my mom was making snacks.

2. Those math problems have been written in my notebook.

3. I could have played outside until sundown.

4. Have you ever read this classic book?

5. We should climb to the top of the hill.

Circle the main verb and underline the helping verb or verbs in each sentence.

6. This summer we have been staying in Washington, D.C.

7. This city can be a very interesting place.

8. Did you visit all of the Smithsonian museums?

9. I have seen a copy of the Declaration of Independence.

10. How far in the air does the Washington Monument rise?

11. Guides were showing people around the White House.

12. You may view a variety of historical artifacts and portraits.

13. The White House has been changed by each new president.

Write a sentence for each verb phrase.

14. can be found

_____

15. could have been

_____

16. has taken

_____

17. might learn

_____

For additional help, review pages 82–83 in your textbook or visit www.voyagesinenglish.com.

4.2 Verb Phrases

A **verb phrase** is a group of words that does the work of a single verb. A verb phrase contains a main verb and one or more **helping verbs.** In questions and some statements, the parts of the verb phrase may be separated.

Use the helping verbs in the box to complete the verb phrase in each sentence.

might	did	could	has	were	have been

1. The rain forests **have been** disappearing slowly over the years.
2. _____ you know that these forests provide oxygen to the atmosphere?
3. If our class goes to the museum, I _____ visit a rain forest biome.
4. Rain forests _____ continue to shrink in size if we're not careful.
5. The loss of the trees _____ affected the animals that live in the forests.
6. We _____ taking notes about many of these rain forest facts.

Use each word as part of a verb phrase in a sentence.

7. boiling _____
8. enjoy _____
9. read _____
10. become _____
11. invent _____
12. eating _____
13. cut _____

Circle whether the underlined part in each sentence is a main verb (MV), a helping verb (HV), or a verb phrase (VP).

14. Many varieties of shoes <u>are</u> displayed at the factory outlet.   MV   HV   VP
15. Sheila <u>can be found</u> at the place almost every day.   MV   HV   VP
16. <u>Have</u> you <u>been</u> shopping at this location today?   MV   HV   VP
17. My mom has <u>made</u> some great deals there.   MV   HV   VP
18. My parents and I are <u>going</u> there this weekend.   MV   HV   VP

For additional help, review pages 82–83 in your textbook or visit www.voyagesinenglish.com.

4.3　Principal Parts of Verbs

A verb has **four principal parts:** the **present,** the **present participle,** the **past,** and the **past participle.** The present participle is formed by adding *-ing* to the present. The past and past participle are formed by adding *-d* or *-ed*.

Complete the chart.

PRESENT	PRESENT PARTICIPLE	PAST	PAST PARTICIPLE
1. cook	_____	_____	_____
2. survive	_____	_____	_____
3. jog	_____	_____	_____
4. laugh	_____	_____	_____
5. cry	_____	_____	_____
6. chop	_____	_____	_____
7. type	_____	_____	_____

Write whether each verb in italics is *present* or *present participle*.

8. Maria and I were *talking* after dinner. _____

9. Her sister *works* at the clothing store. _____

10. Maria *visits* her grandmother on Wednesdays. _____

11. She is *visiting* to keep her company and to read to her. _____

12. Maria's grandmother *smiles* when she sees her. _____

13. Maria is *taking* some freshly baked bread with her. _____

14. Her grandmother's neighbors *call* Maria an angel. _____

Write whether each verb in italics is *past* or *past participle*.

15. Michael *asked* Katrina for help with his homework. _____

16. Michael and Katrina *studied* all afternoon. _____

17. Katrina has *explored* the entire library. _____

18. She has *looked* everywhere for a particular book. _____

19. Even her friends have *tried* to help her find a copy. _____

20. Katrina later *located* the book on the Internet. _____

21. Michael had *remained* behind to study for a math test. _____

For additional help, review pages 84–85 in your textbook or visit www.voyagesinenglish.com.

4.3 Principal Parts of Verbs

A verb has **four principal parts:** the **present,** the **present participle,** the **past,** and the **past participle.** The present participle is formed by adding *-ing* to the present. The past and past participle are formed by adding *-d* or *-ed*.

Complete each sentence with the form of the verb in parentheses.

1. Ms. Takagawa _____ the students extra credit for their reports. (offer—past)

2. The chef is _____ her famous meat loaf. (make—present participle)

3. The mechanic has _____ more oil to the engine. (add—past participle)

4. That baking lasagna _____ so delicious. (smell—present)

5. While Tony set the table, Maria _____ the salad. (toss—past)

6. The workers _____ the room for a new coat of paint. (prepare—past)

7. Sherona and I have _____ little shells around the frame. (glue—past participle)

Write whether each underlined verb is *present, present participle, past,* or *past participle.*

8. The nurse <u>helped</u> her patient up the stairs. _____

9. Several rabbits have <u>hopped</u> right past the garden gate. _____

10. Jason <u>races</u> his bike over the course like a pro. _____

11. His thoroughbred is <u>racing</u> past any of the other horses. _____

12. We <u>watch</u> this program every day. _____

13. A group of children is <u>helping</u> us clean up the park. _____

14. The audience <u>appreciates</u> the new collection of artwork. _____

15. Richard <u>named</u> his new hamster Peanut. _____

Write a sentence for each verb using the verb form in parentheses.

16. sweep (present participle)

_____

17. serve (present)

_____

18. explore (past)

_____

For additional help, review pages 84–85 in your textbook or visit www.voyagesinenglish.com.

© Loyola Press. Voyages in English Grade 5

Section 4 • 55

4.4 Irregular Verbs

The simple past and the past participle of irregular verbs do not end in *-ed*. These parts of irregular verbs take a variety of forms.

Complete the chart.

PRESENT	PAST	PAST PARTICIPLE
1. come	_____	_____
2. teach	_____	_____
3. give	_____	_____
4. see	_____	_____
5. have	_____	_____
6. begin	_____	_____
7. bring	_____	_____

Complete each sentence with the past or the past participle of the irregular verb in parentheses.

8. Mrs. Renquist _____ me how to play the piano. (teach)

9. When Dan was getting ready for bed, a mosquito _____ him. (bite)

10. The driver _____ the package on the front porch. (leave)

11. All the leaves have _____ from the trees after that first storm. (fall)

12. I had _____ a poem about the falling snow. (write)

13. The teacher was surprised that nobody _____ the answer. (know)

14. Delaney _____ six laps during swim practice. (swim)

15. They _____ in line for an hour to get tickets for the show. (stand)

Write a sentence for each verb, using the form in parentheses.

16. hurt (past) _____

17. do (past participle) _____

18. build (past) _____

19. dig (past participle) _____

20. give (past participle) _____

21. buy (past) _____

© Loyola Press. Voyages in English   Grade 5

For additional help, review pages 86–87 in your textbook or visit www.voyagesinenglish.com.

4.5 More Irregular Verbs

The simple past and the past participle of irregular verbs do not end in *-ed*. These parts of irregular verbs take a variety of forms.

Complete the chart.

PRESENT	PRESENT PARTICIPLE	PAST	PAST PARTICIPLE
1. do	_____	_____	_____
2. break	_____	_____	_____
3. swim	_____	_____	_____
4. go	_____	_____	_____
5. see	_____	_____	_____
6. take	_____	_____	_____

Write the correct form of the verb in parentheses to complete each sentence.

7. Ethan _____ his arm while skateboarding yesterday. (break)

8. The Tanners _____ to Florida for a week last winter. (go)

9. My family is _____ to the mountains for our vacation. (go)

10. Tina _____ a dance class to improve her balance. (take)

11. Lisa is _____ Spanish lessons after school. (take)

12. Nate has _____ the monarch butterfly migration twice. (see)

13. With so many free throws, Nick has _____ the school record. (break)

14. Chad _____ a book about rugby. (choose)

15. His homemade boat _____ as soon as he put it in the water. (sink)

Write a sentence for each verb, using the form in parentheses.

16. go (past participle) _____

17. do (past) _____

18. see (present participle) _____

19. fall (past participle) _____

20. say (past) _____

21. sink (past participle) _____

22. take (past) _____

For additional help, review pages 88–89 in your textbook or visit www.voyagesinenglish.com.

Section 4 • 57

4.6 Simple Tenses

The **simple present tense** tells about something that is true or that happens again and again. The **simple past tense** tells about an action that happens in the past. The **future tense** tells about an action that will happen in the future.

Underline the verb or verb phrase in each sentence. Write whether the tense of each is *simple present*, *simple past*, or *future*.

1. Silver dolphins leaped through the waves. _____

2. The turtles will crawl up onto the beach. _____

3. Do you see that big wave? _____

4. Maya will surf every weekend this summer. _____

5. Jellyfish gathered in the shallow water. _____

6. Tourists often watch whales from that boat. _____

7. Amanda jumped in and out of the waves. _____

8. Tomorrow we will try our new surfboards. _____

9. Jonathan won a surfing contest last week. _____

10. Charlie cooked hot dogs over the campfire. _____

11. We eat potato salad at every picnic. _____

12. Several people made a sand castle. _____

13. Andy will use the fins and the snorkel tomorrow. _____

14. Children played in the sand next to the surf. _____

15. After the trip he will show the video to us. _____

Write a sentence for each verb in the tense in parentheses.

16. swim (simple past)

_____

17. play (simple present)

_____

18. float (future)

_____

19. develop (simple present)

_____

© Loyola Press. Voyages in English Grade 5

For additional help, review pages 90–91 in your textbook or visit www.voyagesinenglish.com.

4.7   Progressive Tenses

The **present progressive tense** tells what is happening now. The **past progressive tense** tells what was happening in the past. The **future progressive tense** tells about something that will be happening in the future.

Write whether each underlined verb phrase is in the *present progressive*, the *past progressive*, or the *future progressive* tense.

1. Amanda <u>is singing</u> in the school choir.   _____

2. Many singers <u>will be performing</u> in the Holiday Show.   _____

3. Hopeful participants <u>were auditioning</u> for the show.   _____

4. Terence <u>is dancing</u> with a group of people.   _____

5. Jody <u>will be playing</u> the violin with the orchestra.   _____

Complete each sentence with the form of the verb in parentheses.

6. Jamal _____ soccer earlier. (play—past progressive)

7. Ana _____ Spanish before her trip. (study—present progressive)

8. Sarah _____ me later. (help—future progressive)

9. Horses _____ through the field. (gallop—past progressive)

10. Their parents _____ a vacation. (plan—present progressive)

11. A tiny kitten _____ in her lap. (sleep—present progressive)

12. Lizanne _____ the national anthem. (sing—future progressive)

Write two sentences for each verb. Use the present progressive tense in the first sentence and the past progressive tense in the second sentence.

13. compete _____

_____

14. eat _____

_____

15. look _____

_____

16. enjoy _____

_____

For additional help, review pages 92–93 in your textbook
or visit www.voyagesinenglish.com.

Section 4 • 59

4.8 Present Perfect Tense

The **present perfect tense** uses the past participle and a form of *have* (*have* or *has*). The present perfect tense tells about an action that started in the past and continues into the present time.

Underline the verb phrase in the present perfect tense in each sentence.

1. Dragonflies have lived on Earth for 300 million years.
2. I have read an interesting book about the life of cowboys.
3. Marisa has played the violin since the age of four.
4. Eric, have you cleaned your room yet?
5. Kenneth has left his baseball glove at home.
6. Many animals have developed camouflage as a form of defense.
7. I have taught myself chess.
8. Has Judith joined the poetry club?
9. The children have been in the park all morning.
10. My cousins have taken karate lessons.

Complete each sentence with the present perfect tense of the verb in parentheses.

11. Tom _____ many coins buried under the couch cushions. (find)
12. Andy's sisters _____ volleyball. (play)
13. My grandfather _____ a small plane across the country. (fly)
14. The famous athlete _____ in the marathon for many years. (run)
15. This rainstorm _____ the worst one I can remember. (be)
16. The twins _____ their keys again. (lose)

Write a sentence using each verb in the present perfect tense.

17. bring _____
18. open _____
19. pack _____
20. grow _____
21. clean _____
22. try _____

For additional help, review pages 94–95 in your textbook or visit www.voyagesinenglish.com.

4.9 Past Perfect Tense

The **past perfect tense** tells about a past action that was completed before another past action started. The past perfect tense is formed by using *had* and the past participle of the verb.

Underline the verb phrase in the past perfect tense in each sentence.

1. Mrs. Evans had taken a French class before she traveled to Paris.

2. By the time we reached the end of the trail, we had hiked nearly six miles.

3. Jonah had finished his chores before the tournament at the miniature golf park.

4. The cheerleaders had learned two new routines by the second game of the season.

5. Someone had found the keys under the dining room table.

6. Before we moved to California, I had never seen the ocean.

7. Once we had arrived at the beach, we realized our swimsuits were still at home.

8. We had not known that sand dollars were real animals until we found one.

Complete each sentence with the past perfect tense of the verb in parentheses.

9. I raised my hand once I _____ the answer. (identify)

10. After Tracy _____ the spicy ribs, she asked for a second helping. (eat)

11. Before Manuel gave his speech, he _____ many times. (practice)

12. After they _____ a mess in the kitchen, the children cleaned it up. (make)

13. By the end of her speech, Pat _____ me to vote for her. (convince)

14. Before Ricky got a bicycle, he _____ to school every day. (walk)

15. I _____ to go to the camping store, but we ran out of time. (want)

16. After I _____ my homework, I went out to finish my birdhouse. (do)

Write a sentence using the past perfect tense of each verb.

17. organize _____

18. decorate _____

19. use _____

20. choose _____

21. want _____

22. sing _____

For additional help, review pages 96–97 in your textbook or visit www.voyagesinenglish.com.

Section 4 • 61

4.10 Future Perfect Tense

The **future perfect tense** is used to talk about a future event that will be started and completed before another future event begins. It is formed by using *will have* and the past participle.

Underline the verb phrase in the future perfect tense in each sentence.

1. By Friday afternoon we will have finished another week of school.
2. Dad will have packed the car by the time we get home.
3. The tour guide will have arranged the group's lodging.
4. By the time we leave, Isabella will have fed her fish and turtle.
5. Mom will have made several snacks for the long drive.

Complete each sentence with the future perfect tense of the verb in parentheses.

6. These muffins _____ by dinner. (cool)
7. The performance _____ by noon. (begin)
8. The special event _____ by five o'clock. (end)
9. Our group _____ our reports before the end of class. (finish)
10. By noon they _____ baseball for three hours. (play)
11. Mr. Thomas _____ the garage by Monday. (paint)
12. Hopefully, we _____ home before the storm hits. (arrive)
13. By next week all students _____ their work. (present)
14. They _____ their rooms before they go outside. (clean)
15. The cast _____ all their lines by opening night. (learn)

Write a sentence using the future perfect tense for each verb.

16. decide _____

_____

17. tell _____

_____

18. eat _____

_____

© Loyola Press. Voyages in English Grade 5

For additional help, review pages 98–99 in your textbook or visit www.voyagesinenglish.com.

SECTION 5   Daily Maintenance

5.1 **A strong wind is blowing the leaves.**
1. What is the complete subject?   _____
2. What is the direct object?   _____
3. What is the verb phrase?   _____
4. Diagram the sentence here.

5.2 **Which computer is more expensive?**
1. Which word is the interrogative adjective?   _____
2. Which word is the comparative adjective?   _____
3. Which word is a linking verb?   _____
4. Diagram the sentence here.

5.3 **Mrs. Hughes has graded our quizzes.**
1. What is the proper noun?   _____
2. Is the proper noun singular or plural?   _____
3. Is the participle present tense or past tense?   _____
4. Diagram the sentence here.

5.4 **Mother's vase was delicate.**
1. Which word is a possessive noun?
2. Is this word singular or plural?
3. Which word describes *vase*?
4. Diagram the sentence here.

_____

_____

_____

5.5 **The band will perform a new song.**
1. Which words are articles?
2. What is the adjective?
3. Is the verb present tense or future tense?
4. Diagram the sentence here.

_____

_____

_____

5.1 Adverbs of Time, Place, and Manner

An **adverb** describes a verb. An **adverb of time** answers the question *when* or *how often*. An **adverb of place** answers the question *where*. An **adverb of manner** answers the question *how*.

Write whether the italicized adverb in each sentence indicates *time*, *place*, or *manner*.

1. The storm clouds *silently* gathered in the sky.   _____

2. A farmer *always* watches the weather.   _____

3. He knew the wind and rain would arrive *soon*.   _____

4. He fed the cows and settled them *inside*.   _____

5. After the farmer put everything away, the rain *finally* came.   _____

Underline the adverb in each sentence. Write whether the adverb is an adverb of *time*, *place*, or *manner*.

6. Marcus finished his work early.   _____

7. Everyone was quiet here during the test.   _____

8. Nine students answered all the questions correctly.   _____

9. Soon the bell will ring for recess.   _____

10. The students ran outside to the playground.   _____

Write whether each adverb indicates *time*, *place*, or *manner*. Then write a sentence for each adverb.

11. above _____

_____

12. tomorrow _____

_____

13. swiftly _____

_____

14. now _____

_____

15. upstairs _____

_____

For additional help, review pages 106–107 in your textbook
or visit www.voyagesinenglish.com.

Section 5 • 67

5.2 Adverbs That Compare

The **positive degree** of an adverb is the base form. It describes one action. The **comparative degree** is used to compare two actions. The **superlative degree** is used to compare three or more actions.

Write the comparative and superlative degrees of each adverb.

	COMPARATIVE	SUPERLATIVE
1. quickly	_____	_____
2. late	_____	_____
3. likely	_____	_____
4. soon	_____	_____
5. politely	_____	_____
6. silently	_____	_____
7. skillfully	_____	_____

Underline the adverb in each sentence. Circle whether the adverb is in the comparative (*C*) or the superlative (*S*) degree.

8. The one who runs fastest will win the race. C S

9. Jason and Emily were less likely to win because they both fell at the start. C S

10. Peter ran more smoothly than the others because of his long legs. C S

11. The crowd yelled most loudly during the 100-yard dash. C S

12. The event staff stayed the latest of everyone to put things away. C S

13. They worked harder than ever to get things done. C S

14. The event posters were stored most carefully so they could be used next year. C S

Write a sentence using each adverb. Use the degree in parentheses.

15. gracefully (comparative)

_____

16. swiftly (superlative)

_____

17. long (superlative)

_____

For additional help, review pages 108–109 in your textbook or visit www.voyagesinenglish.com.

5.5   Adverb Clauses

A **dependent clause** does not express a complete thought. In a sentence it is used together with an **independent clause,** which does express a complete thought. An **adverb clause** is a dependent clause that is used as an adverb.

Underline the adverb clause in each sentence. Circle the conjunction.

1. While we were biking, the rain began to fall.
2. I have not been to the beach since I twisted my ankle.
3. As soon as she finishes her homework, Lisa can go with her friends.
4. Mom will not let us play until we finish our chores.
5. As long as the snow keeps falling, school will be canceled.
6. After the storm ended, my friends and I went sledding.
7. We cannot see the basketball hoop when it gets dark.
8. Dylan gets nervous whenever he makes a speech.

Use a conjunction from the box to complete the adverb clause in each sentence.

when	until	after	before	now	while

9. _____ I go to the store, I always get a new magazine.
10. I won't be able to research my topic _____ I get home.
11. He met his friends _____ he finished his homework.
12. _____ we left for the weekend, I cleaned my room and packed.
13. _____ that we are here, I can go fishing.
14. I glued letters on the poster _____ my partner cut out pictures.

Complete each sentence with an adverb clause.

15. I usually go to the park _____.
16. Our family left for the game _____.
17. Ryan bought a new book _____.
18. Shane will do his homework _____.
19. Our neighbor moved to Ohio _____.
20. The Swensons found a family heirloom _____.

For additional help, review pages 114–115 in your textbook or visit www.voyagesinenglish.com.

Section 5 • 71

5.5 | Adverb Clauses

A **dependent clause** does not express a complete thought. In a sentence it is used together with an **independent clause,** which does express a complete thought. An **adverb clause** is a dependent clause that is used as an adverb.

Write a conjunction to complete the adverb clause in each sentence.

1. _____ our teacher erased the board, we knew there would be a test.

2. Carlos shouted with excitement _____ Julie hit a home run.

3. The skaters will compete _____ the ice is cleaned.

4. _____ the other team performed, we stretched and prepared.

5. We couldn't go to the movies tonight _____ Dad had to work late.

6. _____ there is thunder, his sister hides her head under a pillow.

7. Sophie has made many friends _____ her family moved to town.

8. The roast won't be ready _____ the timer rings.

9. Their class will take the field trip _____ they have raised enough money.

10. Sherry wanted to finish the assignment _____ the bell rang.

Complete each sentence with an adverb clause. Circle the conjunction.

11. The wind created huge waves _____.

12. Matt finished the book _____.

13. _____, the dog show was over.

14. Ally found a sweatshirt _____.

15. _____, I saw many butterflies.

16. Sam wrote his paper _____.

17. _____, our team met for practice.

Use each conjunction to write a sentence with an adverb clause.

18. while _____

19. after _____

20. before _____

21. until _____

22. whenever _____

© Loyola Press. Voyages in English   **Grade 5**

For additional help, review pages 114–115 in your textbook or visit www.voyagesinenglish.com.

SECTION 6 Daily Maintenance

6.1 **Valerie quickly solved the math problem.**
1. Which word is a proper noun?
2. What is the simple predicate?
3. Which noun is used as an adjective?
4. Diagram the sentence here.

_____
_____
_____

6.2 **A silver jet is flying overhead.**
1. What is the complete subject?
2. What is the verb phrase?
3. Which word is an adverb?
4. Diagram the sentence here.

_____
_____
_____

6.3 **He never forgets his homework.**
1. Is *He* an object pronoun or a subject pronoun?
2. What is the possessive adjective?
3. Which word is an adverb?
4. Diagram the sentence here.

_____
_____
_____

6.4 **Their sister plays the piano well.**
1. Is the verb present tense or past tense?
2. Which word is the direct object?
3. Which word is an adverb?
4. Diagram the sentence here.

_____
_____
_____

6.5 **I lost my backpack again.**
1. What is the complete subject?   _____
2. Is the verb regular or irregular?   _____
3. Which word is an adverb of time?   _____
4. Diagram the sentence here.

6.6 **This novel is very long.**
1. Which word is a linking verb?   _____
2. What is the subject complement?   _____
3. Which word is an adverb of degree?   _____
4. Diagram the sentence here.

6.2 Prepositional Phrases as Adjectives

A preposition and its object, along with any words that describe the object, form a **prepositional phrase.** A prepositional phrase used as an adjective is called an **adjective phrase.** It describes a noun or a pronoun.

Complete each sentence with a prepositional phrase from the box.

by Sam Wright	on the farm	in his home	from Virginia
about the festival	in the park	from the store	of summer camp

1. I just finished a new book _____.
2. Did you know that eight men _____ became presidents?
3. Many rooms _____ were painted plain white.
4. Tractors _____ are used to plant and harvest wheat.
5. The receipt _____ is lying on the counter.
6. Mr. Jesse asked me to hand out flyers _____.
7. The new tennis courts _____ were installed last year.
8. My father's memories _____ are fun to hear.

Underline the adjective phrase in each sentence. Circle the noun the adjective phrase describes.

9. The meows of the cat were loud.
10. Our hike to the peak was long and difficult.
11. This brochure about local wild animals is informative.
12. A snake in the bushes hissed at us.
13. The opening of the cave was dark and scary.
14. Our picnic under the trees was a great way to spend the day.

Write a sentence using each adjective phrase.

15. from the basement

_____

16. across the ocean

_____

For additional help, review pages 122–123 in your textbook
or visit www.voyagesinenglish.com.

Section 6 • 77

6.2 Prepositional Phrases as Adjectives

A preposition and its object, along with any words that describe the object, form a **prepositional phrase.** A prepositional phrase used as an adjective is called an **adjective phrase.** It describes a noun or a pronoun.

Write the letter of the prepositional phrase in Column B that best completes each sentence in Column A.

COLUMN A	COLUMN B
1. My brother asked a question _____	a. above the treetops.
2. We listened for the honk _____	b. for math class.
3. He has painted many homes _____	c. of the rain forest.
4. Scientists studied animals _____	d. with goat cheese.
5. The shadow was an owl _____	e. about every single problem.
6. David has finished his work _____	f. of the migrating ducks.
7. The salad was roasted beets _____	g. in our town.

Rewrite each sentence. Change the italicized word to an adjective phrase.

8. The *wooden* boat needs repairs and new paint.

_____

9. The canoe trip into the wilderness was led by the *camp* director.

_____

10. Mom's favorite *marble* statues were handcrafted by an artist.

_____

11. We were offered a discount by the *shop* owner.

_____

Write an adjective phrase to complete each sentence.

12. The bike _____ is stored in the garage.

13. He had many questions _____.

14. She noticed the box _____.

15. Many buildings _____ were built before 1900.

16. Their vacation _____ was the best one they have ever had.

© Loyola Press. Voyages in English   Grade 5

For additional help, review pages 122–123 in your textbook or visit www.voyagesinenglish.com.

6.3 Prepositional Phrases as Adverbs

Prepositional phrases used as adverbs are called **adverb phrases.** An adverb phrase generally describes or tells more about a verb. An adverb phrase answers the question *where, when,* or *how.*

Complete each sentence with a prepositional phrase from the box.

with Lawrence	to the top	in her own home	from the sun
on the beach	onto the boat	with enthusiasm	into the pool

1. After just a few hours, the paper faded _____.

2. Adam shared his lunch _____.

3. The huge waves crashed _____.

4. I raced Andy _____ of the stairs.

5. Jenna takes piano lessons _____.

6. Mr. Chandler shook my hand _____ after I found his dog.

7. At the count of three, we all dove _____.

8. Robert and I carried all the fishing equipment _____.

Underline the adverb phrase in each sentence. Circle the word the adverb phrase describes.

9. The deer jumped over the fence.

10. We ran toward the bus stop so we could catch the bus.

11. Marie handled the microscope with great care.

12. Some pioneers crossed the prairie on foot.

13. Our plane departed the airport in the afternoon.

14. The tourists watched the sun set over the Rocky Mountains.

Write a sentence using each adverb phrase.

15. in the afternoon _____

16. near a river _____

17. to a movie _____

18. down the hill _____

For additional help, review pages 124–125 in your textbook or visit www.voyagesinenglish.com.

Section 6 • 79

6.3 Prepositional Phrases as Adverbs

Prepositional phrases used as adverbs are called **adverb phrases.** An adverb phrase generally describes or tells more about a verb. An adverb phrase answers the question *where, when,* or *how.*

Write the letter of the adverb phrase in Column B that completes each sentence in Column A.

COLUMN A		COLUMN B
1. Ryan hit the ball	_____	a. through the icy intersection.
2. We waded up the creek	_____	b. by the doctor.
3. Dad drove carefully	_____	c. out of the stadium.
4. Sometimes my dogs act	_____	d. like puppies.
5. Readers learn a lesson	_____	e. from the beginning.
6. The cast was applied	_____	f. against the current.
7. It is best to tell a story	_____	g. from the moral of the story.

Rewrite each sentence. Change the italicized word to an adverb phrase.

8. The border collie herded the sheep *skillfully*.

_____

9. The ship headed *southward*.

_____

10. The ballerina danced *gracefully* on the stage.

_____

11. I climbed the flight of stairs *effortlessly*.

_____

Write an adverb phrase to complete each sentence.

12. The road crew scheduled a break _____ .

13. We spotted several otters _____ .

14. After dinner was finished, we decided to go _____ .

15. He studied _____ to prepare for his test.

16. The children made dinner _____ while their parents relaxed.

© Loyola Press. Voyages in English   Grade 5

For additional help, review pages 124–125 in your textbook or visit www.voyagesinenglish.com.

6.4 Coordinating Conjunctions

A **conjunction** is a word that connects words or groups of words. A **coordinating conjunction** connects words or groups of words that are of equal importance in a sentence.

Circle the conjunction in each sentence. Underline the words the conjunction connects.

1. Alaska and Hawaii are states.

2. The students to ask are Mia and Luke.

3. Mom baked bread and roasted potatoes.

4. Brandon or Mike will help us move.

5. My puppy chews bones and old shoes.

6. After school we saw a movie and ate dinner.

7. We bought a sandwich and a salad for lunch.

8. The coach or his assistant can start the race.

Underline the conjunction in each sentence. Circle whether the conjunction connects subjects (*S*) or predicates (*P*).

9. Ducks and geese swam in the lagoon.   S P

10. A dragonfly buzzed past but hovered over a bush.   S P

11. Two fish hid under rocks or darted from danger in the water.   S P

12. The sun and wind made sparkling ripples on the water.   S P

13. The smell of the cut grass tickled and teased my nose.   S P

14. An abundance of flowers bloom and decorate the yard.   S P

15. The sights, sounds, and smells are the best part of summer.   S P

Underline the conjunction in each sentence. Circle whether the conjunction connects direct objects (*DO*), subject complements (*SC*), or sentences (*S*).

16. The first snowfall covers the trees and shrubs with a white coat.   DO SC S

17. The snow that fell last night is heavy and deep.   DO SC S

18. We can sit near the fire, or you can cuddle up with a blanket.   DO SC S

19. Bundling up in layers of clothing is bulky but warm.   DO SC S

20. Winter sports can include skiing, skating, and sledding.   DO SC S

For additional help, review pages 126–127 in your textbook or visit www.voyagesinenglish.com.

© Loyola Press. Voyages in English   Grade 5

Section 6 • 81

6.5 Subordinate Conjunctions

A **subordinate conjunction** connects a dependent clause to an independent clause in a sentence. Common subordinate conjunctions include *after*, *as*, *because*, *before*, *once*, *since*, *when*, *whenever*, *while*, and *until*.

Underline the subordinate conjunction in each sentence.

1. A person is not allowed to drive until he or she receives a license.

2. After the rain stopped, earthworms crawled over the wet sidewalk.

3. Ships follow a lighthouse signal whenever they are close to shore.

4. Before we left on the fishing trip, the gear, bait, and snacks were packed.

5. I watched my favorite program once I finished all my homework.

6. While Dad and I cleaned the garage, Mom and Susan raked leaves.

7. Since the sun would set soon, Peter turned on the porch lights.

Circle the subordinate conjunction in each sentence. Then underline the independent clause once and the dependent clause twice.

8. Brett went home because he was not feeling good.

9. We cannot start the baseball game until the rain stops.

10. Once the downpour ended, a rainbow lit up the sky.

11. Students must finish their tests before the bell rings.

12. Let's leave early so we can avoid the worst traffic.

13. I feel very small when I view the enormous, star-filled night sky.

14. Since my friends moved away, I have been lonely.

15. Kayla was only eight years old when she sang her first song onstage.

Write an independent clause to complete each sentence. Then circle the subordinate conjunction.

16. _____

    when I went to the park.

17. Until he knows what to expect,

    _____.

18. _____

    since I'm already home.

© Loyola Press. Voyages in English Grade 5

For additional help, review pages 128–129 in your textbook or visit www.voyagesinenglish.com.

7.5 **Ben and Ezra have reviewed their notes carefully.**
1. Is the verb tense present or past perfect?   _____
2. Is the subject simple or compound?   _____
3. Which word is a coordinating conjunction?   _____
4. Diagram the sentence on another sheet of paper.

7.6 **The movie will begin in eight minutes.**
1. Is the predicate simple or compound?   _____
2. What tense is the verb?   _____
3. What is the prepositional phrase?   _____
4. Diagram the sentence on another sheet of paper.

7.7 **Hers is the drawing of a horse.**
1. Which words are articles?   _____
2. Which word is a possessive pronoun?   _____
3. What is the object of the preposition?   _____
4. Diagram the sentence on another sheet of paper.

7.8 **We washed and waxed the car.**
1. Is the predicate simple or compound?   _____
2. Is the pronoun singular or plural?   _____
3. Which word is a coordinating conjunction?   _____
4. Diagram the sentence on another sheet of paper.

7.9 **Wow! These Indian dresses are exquisite.**
1. Which word is a proper adjective? _____
2. Which word is a demonstrative adjective? _____
3. Which word is an interjection? _____
4. Diagram the sentence on another sheet of paper.

7.10 **They can play when their chores are done.**
1. What is the possessive adjective? _____
2. Is *can* a linking verb or a helping verb? _____
3. Which word is a subordinate conjunction? _____
4. Diagram the sentence on another sheet of paper.

7.11 **Shh! The baby is sleeping peacefully.**
1. What is the verb phrase? _____
2. Which word is an adverb? _____
3. Which word is an interjection? _____
4. Diagram the sentence on another sheet of paper.

7.4 Direct and Indirect Objects

The **direct object** is a noun or a pronoun that answers the question *whom* or *what* after an action verb. The **indirect object** tells to whom, for whom, to what, or for what an action is done.

Underline the direct object and circle the indirect object in each sentence.

1. Marcie sent James the letter.
2. Mom made us dinner.
3. Jamie's uncle sold him the bike.
4. A bird brought its babies some food.
5. My brother sent Aunt Sophie a birthday card.
6. Grandfather left Luis his stamp collection.
7. Alicia assigned the groups the tasks for their projects.
8. Mom made my sister a promise.
9. Julia sent her pen pal the package.
10. At the department store, the salesperson sold me a new sweater.

Write whether each underlined word is a *direct object* or an *indirect object*.

11. Some students earn scholarships.   _____
12. Mr. Slater assigned us a research report.   _____
13. The documentary describes the life of bees.   _____
14. Scientists show world leaders their findings.   _____
15. Yesterday Jennifer gave the class her report.   _____
16. The tour group finally visited Australia.   _____
17. Coastal towns prepare citizens for possible tsunamis. _____

Write a direct object and an indirect object to complete each sentence.

18. The coach teaches _____.
19. A salesclerk offered _____.
20. My friend told _____.
21. Mr. Davis gave _____.
22. Antonio sent _____.

For additional help, review pages 142–143 in your textbook
or visit www.voyagesinenglish.com.

7.5 Subject Complements

A **subject complement** completes the meaning of a linking verb in a sentence. If the subject complement is a noun or a pronoun, it renames the subject. If the subject complement is an adjective, it describes the subject.

Circle the subject complement in each sentence. Then write whether the subject complement is a *noun* or an *adjective*.

1. The boat is also their home.   _____

2. Julio was the only player on the field.   _____

3. My neighbors are volunteers.   _____

4. This historic bridge is very scenic.   _____

5. The portrait of your grandmother is beautiful.   _____

6. Your ankle seems swollen.   _____

7. My favorite sport is volleyball.   _____

8. The choices for sightseeing were numerous.   _____

9. Dylan's accomplishments are well known.   _____

10. He was successful in reaching his goal.   _____

Complete each sentence with a noun or an adjective used as a subject complement.

11. The best winter sport is _____.

12. I am _____ at snowboarding.

13. My friends are _____.

14. Erica was a _____.

15. She will have been _____ by next year.

16. Later Erica and I were _____.

Write a sentence that uses each word as a subject complement.

17. boring _____

18. mammal _____

19. hero _____

20. spectacular _____

21. subject _____

22. heavy _____

For additional help, review pages 144–145 in your textbook or visit www.voyagesinenglish.com.

7.5 Subject Complements

A **subject complement** completes the meaning of a linking verb in a sentence. If the subject complement is a noun or a pronoun, it renames the subject. If the subject complement is an adjective, it describes the subject.

Write *yes* or *no* to identify whether the underlined word is a subject complement.

1. His parents were <u>musicians</u>.   _____
2. His mom taught children <u>piano</u>.   _____
3. My favorite guitar player is <u>Jason Mraz</u>.   _____
4. His band played a concert in <u>Radio City Music Hall</u>.   _____
5. Abbey was a hard <u>worker</u>.   _____
6. She was a <u>student</u> of the music college.   _____
7. She will be a concert <u>pianist</u> some day.   _____
8. The music teacher awarded her a <u>scholarship</u>.   _____
9. She played difficult <u>chords</u> with ease.   _____
10. Her first concert was a huge <u>success</u>.   _____

Underline the subject complement in each sentence. Circle whether the subject complement is a noun (*N*) or an adjective (*A*).

11. She is a Spanish actor.   N   A
12. The repairs to their home were extensive.   N   A
13. This concert was his best performance.   N   A
14. Freshly baked bread smells simply wonderful.   N   A
15. The painting in the museum was a forgery.   N   A
16. Our coach was an inspiration to many people.   N   A

Write four sentences that tell about your family. Use a subject complement in each sentence.

17. _____

18. _____

19. _____

20. _____

© Loyola Press. Voyages in English   Grade 5

For additional help, review pages 144–145 in your textbook or visit www.voyagesinenglish.com.

7.6 Sentence Order

A sentence is in **natural order** when the verb follows the subject. A sentence is in **inverted order** when the main verb or a helping verb comes before the subject.

Write whether each sentence is in _natural_ or _inverted_ order.

1. Across the prairie galloped a herd of wild horses.   _inverted_
2. A large raccoon scurried over the fence.   _natural_
3. Justin's sister took the last piece of cornbread.   _inverted_
4. In what year were you born?   _inverted_
5. Across the horizon drifted ominous storm clouds.   _inverted_
6. The tired hikers rested by the edge of the stream.   _natural_
7. Down tumbled the tower of blocks.   _inverted_
8. The fire engines raced to the scene.   _natural_
9. From the far side of the mountain rose the sun.   _inverted_

Rewrite each sentence, putting it in natural order.

10. Over the bar stretched the high jumper.
    The high jumper stretched over the bar.

11. Out of the runner's hand dropped the baton.
    The baton dropped out of the runner's hand.

12. Around the track sprinted the runners.
    The runners sprinted across the track.

Rewrite each sentence, putting it in inverted order.

13. A majestic eagle soared over the treetops.
    Over the treetops a majestic eagle soared.

14. Freezing rain came from the clouds.
    From the clouds came freezing rain.

15. The northern lights danced through the sky.
    Through the sky danced the northern lights.

For additional help, review pages 146–147 in your textbook or visit www.voyagesinenglish.com.

© Loyola Press. Voyages in English   Grade 5

7.7   Compound Subjects and Predicates

A sentence with two or more subjects is said to have a **compound subject.** Two or more predicates joined by a coordinating conjunction form a **compound predicate.**

Underline the compound simple subjects once and the compound simple predicates twice in each sentence.

1. Quarters or dollars can be used in the vending machine.

2. Hydrogen and oxygen make up a water molecule.

3. Darnell climbed and hiked the mountain trail.

4. Mysteries and fantasies have fascinating plots.

5. This company writes and publishes many best sellers.

6. The crowd cheered and clapped for the amazing stunt.

7. Hockey and golf are my two favorite sports.

8. Matthew earned and saved enough money for the trip.

9. Olivia or her sister will help you with your homework.

10. Chess or art are activities that we can choose.

Circle the correct verb to complete each sentence.

11. The game and the parade (is   are) going to be on TV today.

12. Believe it or not, my dad and mom (like   likes) to watch both.

13. A sled or a toboggan (is   are) available for rental.

14. Chicago or San Francisco (was   were) the site of the concert.

15. Bracelets and necklaces (is   are) for sale at the shop.

16. Laughter and kindness (make   makes) a happy person.

Combine each pair of sentences into one sentence with either a compound subject or a compound predicate.

17. Roses smell wonderful. Roses brighten up a room.

_____

18. A beach can be rocky. A mountain trail can be rocky.

_____

For additional help, review pages 148–149 in your textbook or visit www.voyagesinenglish.com.

Section 7 • 95

7.8 Compound Direct Objects

A verb that has two or more direct objects is said to have a **compound direct object.** Compound direct objects are usually connected by the coordinating conjunction *and* or *or*.

Underline the compound direct objects in each sentence.

1. My family will visit Canada or Alaska this summer.

2. We will take a train and a boat.

3. Should I bring a sweater or a coat?

4. Alexis bought bananas and watermelon at the grocery store.

5. I could use a worm or cheese to catch fish.

6. Forrest had turkey and avocado on his sandwich.

7. We told our family and friends about the party.

8. Each tourist bought a souvenir or a T-shirt at the gift shop.

9. The wind blew drifts and ridges of snow around the buildings.

10. We found our boots and gloves in the trunk.

Complete each sentence with a compound direct object.

11. Mother bought _____ and _____ for the party.

12. Meg placed _____ and _____ on the table.

13. People donated _____ or _____ to the charity.

14. Jennifer and Alma made _____ and _____ .

15. We played _____ or _____ in the park.

16. Dad found a _____ and a _____ in the garage.

17. I studied _____ and _____ at the library.

Write four sentences about things people do on vacation. Use a compound direct object in each sentence.

18. _____

19. _____

20. _____

21. _____

For additional help, review pages 150–151 in your textbook or visit www.voyagesinenglish.com.

7.9 Compound Subject Complements

A verb with two or more subject complements is said to have a **compound subject complement.** Compound subject complements are usually connected by the coordinating conjunction *and* or *or*.

Underline the compound subject complement in each sentence. Circle whether the subject complement is a noun (*N*) or an adjective (*A*).

1. She seemed anxious and excited before her solo.   N   A

2. The English actor is well known and respected.   N   A

3. The only vegetables in the salad were lettuce and radishes.   N   A

4. My favorite fruits are strawberries and watermelon.   N   A

5. The path through the park is long and winding.   N   A

6. Our breakfast was toast and bananas.   N   A

7. The buzzing sound was constant and annoying.   N   A

8. Aunt Peg's cherry pie can be tart or sweet.   N   A

9. Ava's brother is a swimmer and a runner.   N   A

10. The food at the new restaurant could be good or bad.   N   A

11. Juan's favorite movies are comedies and mysteries.   N   A

12. The automobile in the ad was sleek and shiny.   N   A

Write a compound subject complement to complete each sentence.

13. The pancake mix is _____ and _____.

14. I am _____ and _____ about the test today.

15. My sandwich was _____ and _____.

16. Was the principal _____ or _____ by this snowstorm?

17. I am _____ and _____ that I passed the test.

18. Conner was _____ and _____ after practice.

19. Are you _____ or _____ today?

20. Tina's favorite colors are _____ and _____.

21. Bread served with dinner is _____ or _____.

22. My dream vacation destination would be _____ or _____.

For additional help, review pages 152–153 in your textbook
or visit www.voyagesinenglish.com.

7.9 Compound Subject Complements

A verb with two or more subject complements is said to have a **compound subject complement.** Compound subject complements are usually connected by the coordinating conjunction *and* or *or.*

Write *yes* or *no* to identify whether the underlined words are a compound subject complement.

1. He is a basketball <u>player</u> and a <u>businessman</u>.   _____
2. Jose's soccer moves are <u>quick</u> and <u>agile</u>.   _____
3. His other favorite sports are <u>football</u> and <u>baseball</u>.   _____
4. <u>Dad</u> and <u>Mom</u> took the team out for snacks after the game.   _____
5. We took the <u>camera</u> and extra <u>batteries</u> on our trip.   _____
6. The bus driver was <u>polite</u> and <u>helpful</u> when we asked for directions.   _____
7. Mike told <u>Frank</u> and <u>Pierre</u> about the new sailing vacation.   _____
8. The tree fort was <u>sturdy</u> and <u>high</u> above the ground.   _____
9. A rock wall climb is <u>tough</u> and <u>dangerous</u>.   _____
10. Different types of rope are used in <u>climbing</u> and <u>rappelling</u>.   _____

Underline the compound subject complements in each sentence. Circle whether the subject complement is a noun (*N*) or an adjective (*A*).

11. My favorite hockey teams are the Blackhawks and the Canadiens.   N   A
12. Bobby Hull was a player and a commissioner of hockey.   N   A
13. Of all the states, Alaska is the largest but least populated.   N   A
14. According to many people, Hawaii is warm and relaxing.   N   A
15. I am happy and comfortable at home.   N   A

Write a sentence that uses each pair of words as a compound subject complement.

16. famous, respected

_____

17. snow, ice

_____

18. excited, nervous

_____

© Loyola Press. Voyages in English   Grade 5

For additional help, review pages 152–153 in your textbook or visit www.voyagesinenglish.com.

7.10 Compound Sentences

A **compound sentence** contains two or more independent clauses. A compound sentence is formed when two or more independent clauses are connected by the coordinating conjunction *and*, *but*, or *or*.

Underline the complete subject once and the complete predicate twice in each independent clause in these compound sentences.

1. I enjoy many kinds of books, but my brother only likes science fiction.

2. The painting was original and creative; it won first prize.

3. He dusted the shelf, and the books fell over.

4. Grandfather may take a plane, or my father may drive him here.

5. Maurice will not leave until noon, but he should arrive before the start of the game.

6. The edge of the ice rink is banked with snow, and the hockey nets are at each end.

7. The ambulance's siren blared; the cars pulled over.

8. A diamond is the hardest stone, and soapstone is the softest.

9. Freezing air can be unsafe, but wind chills make the air even more dangerous.

10. One group prepared for a hike, and the other group dressed warmly for ice-skating.

Write a compound sentence that combines each pair of sentences. Use a comma before the coordinating conjunction.

11. Safety goggles will protect your eyes. A hard hat will protect your head.

_____

12. One school break is in winter. The longest school break is in summer.

_____

13. Peter ran out of paper. He found some that had fallen behind the printer.

_____

Combine each pair of sentences to form a compound sentence. Use a semicolon.

14. Plants regrow each spring. The warm sun gives them energy.

_____

15. There was a full moon last week. It happens once a month.

_____

For additional help, review pages 154–155 in your textbook or visit www.voyagesinenglish.com.

7.11 Complex Sentences

> A **complex sentence** contains one independent clause and one dependent clause. Dependent clauses that act as adverbs are called **adverb clauses.** An adverb clause can tell when something occurred.

Write whether each clause is _dependent_ or _independent_.

1. Captain Carlos was born in Guadalajara, Mexico _____

2. Before his visit to Puerto Vallarta _____

3. Carlos had always dreamed of the sea _____

4. While he was in elementary school _____

5. When Carlos saw the boat for the first time _____

6. His grin widened from ear to ear _____

7. Since his first trip was on the water _____

8. Fishing was something Carlos always dreamed of doing _____

9. Carlos's father was proud of his son's accomplishments _____

10. After he had his first week at sea _____

Underline the independent clause once and the adverb clause twice in each sentence.

11. After she finished her homework, Janna practiced the piano.

12. When we heard the good news, we jumped for joy.

13. We plan to visit Yellowstone National Park before we travel to California.

14. Since summer ended, Manuel has been waiting for the soccer season.

15. We cannot begin the show until Dana and David arrive.

16. While it was snowing, the children were catching snowflakes on their tongues.

17. We all congratulated the winner after the contest was finished.

Write an adverb clause that tells when to complete each sentence.

18. He received the prize _____ .

19. Jamie talked on the phone _____ .

20. _____ , my family helped me.

21. _____ , the group paid the check and left.

© Loyola Press. Voyages in English   Grade 5

For additional help, review pages 156–157 in your textbook or visit www.voyagesinenglish.com.

7.11 Complex Sentences

A **complex sentence** contains one independent clause and one dependent clause. Dependent clauses that act as adverbs are called **adverb clauses.** An adverb clause can tell when something occurred.

Write *yes* or *no* to identify whether each sentence is a complex sentence.

1. Kaitlin went upstairs after she cleaned the dishes. _____
2. While Jeremy was washing the car, his dog played in the yard. _____
3. Dylan and Jamie raced each other on their skateboards. _____
4. Mount Rushmore has a giant sculpture of four U.S. presidents. _____
5. Mexico has cities in the mountains, but it also has cities along the sea. _____
6. Before we baked the biscuits, we had to mix together all the ingredients. _____
7. Palm trees sway in the ocean breezes. _____
8. Maurice likes to fish since he lives in a town by the ocean. _____
9. When your basket is full, pour the apples into the bin. _____
10. Only the hardiest plants survive in this cold region. _____

Underline the independent clause once and the adverb clause twice in each sentence.

11. Jason was cutting out the figures while I was gluing them to the poster.
12. After we finished, we showed Mom and Dad our presentation.
13. Emma was excited when she found out she made the volleyball team.
14. Before Kristi competed in the show, she spent a few moments reviewing her routine.
15. The crowd hushed as the skater stepped on the ice.
16. When his performance was done, the crowd cheered.
17. Since Zack is older, he is responsible for taking out the garbage.
18. Our class reached its goal after a generous donation from the mayor.

Write three complex sentences that tell about something you have learned in school this year.

19. _____
20. _____
21. _____

For additional help, review pages 156–157 in your textbook or visit www.voyagesinenglish.com.

Section 7 • 101

SECTION 8 Daily Maintenance

8.1 **Our class has learned about Mayan art.**
1. Which word is a collective noun?   _____
2. What is the verb phrase?   _____
3. Is the sentence declarative or imperative? _____
4. Diagram the sentence on another sheet of paper.

8.2 **The tiny puppy is sleeping peacefully in my lap.**
1. Which word is a preposition?   _____
2. Which word is an adverb?   _____
3. What is the simple subject?   _____
4. Diagram the sentence on another sheet of paper.

8.3 **She made this sculpture.**
1. Is the pronoun singular or plural?   _____
2. Which word is a demonstrative adjective? _____
3. What is the complete predicate?   _____
4. Diagram the sentence on another sheet of paper.

8.4 **Jeff sent me a large package.**
1. Which word is an adjective?   _____
2. What tense is the verb?   _____
3. Which word is an indirect object?   _____
4. Diagram the sentence on another sheet of paper.

8.5 **Nate and Nora quickly completed the puzzle.**
  1. Which word is an adverb?   _____
  2. Which word is an article?   _____
  3. What is the compound subject?   _____
  4. Diagram the sentence on another sheet of paper.

8.6 **The winner of the game was she.**
  1. What is the prepositional phrase?   _____
  2. Is *she* a subject or an object pronoun?   _____
  3. What is the subject complement?   _____
  4. Diagram the sentence on another sheet of paper.

8.7 **The scouts in my troop fish and hike.**
  1. Which word is a plural noun?   _____
  2. Which word is a coordinating conjunction?   _____
  3. What is the compound predicate?   _____
  4. Diagram the sentence on another sheet of paper.

8.8 **We will buy peanuts and popcorn.**
  1. Is the subject singular or plural?   _____
  2. What tense is the verb phrase?   _____
  3. Is the direct object simple or compound?   _____
  4. Diagram the sentence on another sheet of paper.

8.9 **Sandra's bedroom is pink and purple.**
1. Is the possessive noun singular or plural?   _____
2. How is the verb *is* used in the sentence?   _____
3. Which part of the sentence is compound?   _____
4. Diagram the sentence on another sheet of paper.

8.10 **The ball is his, and the marbles are mine.**
1. Which words are possessive pronouns?   _____
2. Which words are nouns?   _____
3. Is the sentence simple or compound?   _____
4. Diagram the sentence on another sheet of paper.

8.11 **Which students quietly walked to their seats?**
1. Which word is an interrogative adjective?   _____
2. Which phrase is used as an adverb?   _____
3. Is the subject simple or compound?   _____
4. Diagram the sentence on another sheet of paper.

8.3 Commas with Conjunctions

A **comma** is used before the **coordinating conjunction** *and*, *but*, or *or* when two independent clauses are joined to form a compound sentence. Commas are used in compound sentences but not in compound sentence parts.

Add commas where needed in these sentences. Then circle the conjunctions.

1. Botany is the study of plants and it has been studied since ancient times.

2. Botanists use microscopes to look at plants but I like to look at them in a garden.

3. Plants can be found deep in the sea or they also grow on the highest mountains.

4. Some plants produce cones and these cones protect the seeds.

5. Not all plants contain chlorophyll but most of them do.

6. Some plants are easy to grow and a rubber tree is an example.

7. Most plants require sunlight, water, and carbon dioxide or they will not survive.

Write *yes* or *no* to tell whether each sentence is correct.

8. We want to visit the zoo, but we also want to see that new movie.   _____

9. The ocean waves crashed, and tumbled on the shore.   _____

10. Brianna can go to the party, or she can stay home and study.   _____

11. This museum has many exhibits and attractions for visitors.   _____

12. Tea can be served cold and tea can be served hot.   _____

13. You can find the books in my backpack, or in my locker.   _____

14. Ava practiced the lines a long time, and we hope she gets the part.   _____

15. Many people live in town, but there are others who live in the country.   _____

Rewrite each pair of sentences as a compound sentence.

16. The wind blew hard outside. We were warm inside the house.

    _____

17. My family saw lots of puppies in the shelter. We decided to adopt one.

    _____

18. I may have failed to follow the recipe correctly. Perhaps the oven isn't working.

    _____

For additional help, review pages 166–167 in your textbook or visit www.voyagesinenglish.com.

Section 8 • 107

8.3 Commas with Conjunctions

A **comma** is used before the **coordinating conjunction** *and*, *but*, or *or* when two independent clauses are joined to form a compound sentence. Commas are used in compound sentences but not in compound sentence parts.

Add commas to each sentence. Then circle the letter of the rule you followed to add commas.

> **a.** Use commas to separate words in a series.
> **b.** Use a comma before a conjunction in a compound sentence.

1. It is a cold night and we are not going outside.   a b
2. I like to stay inside when it is windy snowy and dark.   a b
3. Tomorrow we are going skiing or we may go sledding.   a b
4. I'll make sure to pack my gloves hat and scarf.   a b
5. Mom is bringing a lunch and Dad is putting the gear in the car.   a b
6. The sun was shining brightly but the temperature was very cold.   a b
7. I really miss the sunny days hot sand and warm breezes of last summer. a b
8. Jessie and Rick are coming with us and they are bringing a big toboggan. a b
9. Mom Dad and I prepare sandwiches and hot soup.   a b

Rewrite each sentence, adding commas where needed.

10. The marching band has drums horns flags and fancy uniforms.

   _____

11. The football team won their first five games and they are now in first place.

   _____

12. The spectators cheered clapped and whistled after each touchdown.

   _____

Write two sentences, using commas in a series in one sentence and a comma and conjunction in the other sentence.

13. _____

14. _____

© Loyola Press. Voyages in English   Grade 5

For additional help, review pages 166–167 in your textbook or visit www.voyagesinenglish.com.

8.6 Capitalization

The first word of every sentence begins with a capital letter. A proper noun also begins with a capital letter. A proper noun names a particular person, a particular place, or a particular thing.

Rewrite each phrase, adding capital letters where needed.

1. new year's day on monday _____

2. tornadoes over kansas _____

3. democrats vetoed bills _____

4. benefit for the hope foundation _____

5. fell across ridge avenue _____

6. september at parker school _____

7. at mesa state college _____

8. in the forester pavilion _____

Underline each letter that should be capitalized in these sentences.

9. memorial day is the last monday of may each year.

10. veterans day and thanksgiving are in november.

11. i will visit washington, d.c., with my parents this summer.

12. the horse named falling star won the kentucky derby.

13. mr. chang is taking us to the los angeles museum of art on wednesday.

Write a sentence for each topic.

14. your favorite holiday

_____

15. the names of two relatives

_____

16. today's day and date

_____

17. your city and state

_____

For additional help, review pages 172–173 in your textbook or visit www.voyagesinenglish.com.

Section 8 • 111

8.7 Titles of Works

A capital letter begins each important word in the **titles of works.** Titles of books, plays, magazines, movies, and artworks are italicized or underlined. Titles of poems, songs, stories, and articles use quotation marks.

Write *yes* or *no* to tell whether each sentence is correct.

1. My dad subscribes to *Time* magazine. _____

2. We rented The Sound of Music last weekend. _____

3. "Saving the Trees" was an interesting article. _____

4. *Nothin Like a Fifth Grade Crush* is a funny poem. _____

5. Kate DiCamillo wrote the book *The Tale of Despereaux*. _____

6. *Don quixote* is an illustration by Pablo Picasso. _____

7. Shakespeare wrote the famous play *Romeo and Juliet*. _____

Rewrite each title correctly, using capital letters and underlining where needed.

8. *sports illustrated for kids* (magazine) _____

9. "the secret life of killer whales" (article) _____

10. *a comedy of errors* (play) _____

11. "little boy blue" (poem) _____

12. *how a volcano forms* (essay) _____

13. "jewels in the sky" (story) _____

14. *the witch of blackbird pond* (book) _____

15. *ants' nest: an underground city* (book) _____

Write a sentence that includes a title for each topic.

16. Your favorite movie

_____

17. Your favorite book

_____

18. Your favorite song

_____

© Loyola Press. Voyages in English **Grade 5**

For additional help, review pages 174–175 in your textbook or visit www.voyagesinenglish.com.

8.8 Other Uses of Capitalization

Capital letters are used for the first word in a direct quotation, the directions
North, South, East, and West (when they refer to specific regions), the pronoun
I, titles that precede a person's name, and the initials in a person's name.

Rewrite each phrase, using the correct capitalization.

1. fall colors in the north _____

2. president george washington _____

3. a poem by t. s. eliot _____

4. "this is the start of the end" _____

5. my sister and i _____

6. the mountains in the west _____

7. mr. thomas a. williams _____

Rewrite each name, using an initial for the middle name.

8. Jonathan Thomas Brenner _____

9. Jeffrey Steven Chandler _____

10. Ms. Jolayna Marie Kinney _____

11. Ryoko June Liu _____

12. Sandra Davis McMahon _____

13. Alice Annabel Mooney _____

Rewrite each sentence, using capital letters where needed. Use underlining for italicized words.

14. Miss hodges instructed, "be sure to drink plenty of water on your hike."

_____

15. this article, written by Joseph baines, was published last march.

_____

16. Ulrich, who was born in germany, traveled the united states last summer.

_____

17. "can we plan a trip to the museum of science and industry?" asked Mr. James.

_____

For additional help, review pages 176–177 in your textbook
or visit www.voyagesinenglish.com.

Section 8 • 113

8.9 Abbreviations

An **abbreviation** is a shortened form of a word. Capital letters are used for abbreviations when capital letters would be used if the words were written in full. Metric system abbreviations do not use capital letters or periods.

Write the abbreviation for each word.

1. Doctor _____
2. pound _____
3. Street _____
4. Mister _____
5. inch _____
6. hour _____
7. Idaho _____
8. August _____
9. gram _____
10. foot _____

11. December _____
12. ounce _____
13. California _____
14. before noon _____
15. centimeter _____
16. Road _____
17. Governor _____
18. Illinois _____
19. South Dakota _____
20. after noon _____

Rewrite each phrase, using abbreviations for the italicized words.

21. 1211 Main *Street* _____
22. Saturday, *February* 23 _____
23. Denver, *Colorado* _____
    20 *ounces* of cheese _____
    Missus Tamara Davis _____

an answer to each question. Use at least one abbreviation in your answer.

ow many feet are in one yard?

_____

27. In what city and state do you live?

_____

28. What is today's date?

_____

© Loyola Press. Voyages in English   Grade 5

For additional help, review pages 178–179 in your textbook or visit www.voyagesinenglish.com.

8.10 Direct Quotations

A **direct quotation** is the exact words a person has spoken. A direct quotation is enclosed in quotation marks and is separated from the rest of the sentence by one or more commas. Use a capital letter for the first word in a quotation.

Add the quotation marks, commas, and end punctuation where needed in these sentences.

1. Julie pleaded "Can someone help me find my jacket?"

2. "The difference," Mr. Janus said "is the reason we choose."

3. "This is the warmest day we've had this year" said Peter.

4. Mary Jane asked, "Haven't you ever seen a peacock

5. "Fantastic!" shouted Emily, These shoes are just what I want.

6. Collin said, "I've been studying, and I am ready to take the test

Rewrite each sentence, adding quotation marks, commas, end punctuation, and capital letters where needed.

7. look out for that falling branch! i shouted from across the yard.

   _____

8. mr taylor added please have your homework done by friday.

   _____

9. do you think you can finish the hike the camp ranger asked.

   _____

10. well Miranda replied i would like to at least give it a try

   _____

11. wow Terrell exclaimed that building is really tall

   _____

12. Put your muddy boots on the porch Sam's mother instructed.

   _____

13. Gina asked will we be on time for the movie

   _____

14. did you say turn left on first avenue

   _____

For additional help, review pages 180–181 in your textbook or visit www.voyagesinenglish.com.

Section 8 • 115

8.10 Direct Quotations

A **direct quotation** is the exact words a person has spoken. A direct quotation is enclosed in quotation marks and is separated from the rest of the sentence by one or more commas. Use a capital letter for the first word in a quotation.

Add quotation marks to each direct quotation.

1. Shh! I whispered, We don't want to wake her up, do we?

2. I know you don't agree, Mark, but can you understand my point? asked his father.

3. It takes 24 hours for Earth to rotate once, explained the astronomer.

4. Did you know that Saturn has 18 moons? questioned Amy.

5. Dad bought a telescope to look at the constellations, said Jermaine.

6. This bracelet uses a hook, and this necklace clasps with a magnet, explained the jeweler.

7. Twist the rope over itself around the pole and then pull tight, instructed David.

8. Look through the binoculars, said Brock, and you'll get a closer look at the whales.

9. Mrs. Dunning said, Let me know if you have trouble, and I'll give you a hand.

Write a direct quotation to complete each sentence. Use the correct punctuation.

10. _____ said my teacher.

11. His friend yelled, _____

12. _____ asked Mr. Lerner.

13. Amy shouted, _____

14. _____ explained the lab tech.

15. Dylan surprisingly said, _____

16. The child giggled, _____

17. _____ replied Jillian.

Write four sentences that each include a direct quotation.

18. _____

19. _____

20. _____

21. _____

© Loyola Press. Voyages in English   Grade 5

For additional help, review pages 180–181 in your textbook or visit www.voyagesinenglish.com.

8.11 Addresses and Letters

Addresses and letters follow certain capitalization and punctuation rules. Remember these rules when you write addresses and letters.

Rewrite the following, adding capital letters and punctuation where needed. Use abbreviations where possible.

1. 1995 mulberry avenue

   _____

2. dear mister novak:

   _____

3. very truly yours

   _____

4. frankfort michigan 49635

   _____

5. dear uncle raymond

   _____

Rewrite each address correctly.

6. samuel andrews

   3454 eighth street

   grand island, nebraska 68801

   _____

   _____

   _____

7. Jennifer ramirez

   1611 Placita El vuelo

   Mission Texas 78572

   _____

   _____

   _____

8. yolanda Bates

   1555 Harlem ave

   new york new york 10001

   _____

   _____

   _____

Circle the mistakes in the letter. Underline the words that should be abbreviated. On another sheet of paper, rewrite the letter correctly.

9.
                                    479 Lighthouse boulevard
                                    Botany Bay. North Carolina 28401
                                    May 5, 20—

Dear grandma Rose

    thank you so much for my presents. i love my sweater, and the leather journal you gave me is beautiful.

                                    all my love

                                    Amy

For additional help, review pages 182–183 in your textbook or visit www.voyagesinenglish.com.

Section 8 • **117**

SECTION 9 | Daily Maintenance

9.1 **Vicky gave me a red bracelet.**
1. Is the subject simple or compound?   _____
2. What is the direct object?   _____
3. What is the indirect object?   _____
4. Diagram the sentence on another sheet of paper.

9.2 **The local orchestra performed well.**
1. Is the verb an action verb or a being verb?   _____
2. Which word is a collective noun?   _____
3. Is *well* an adjective or an adverb?   _____
4. Diagram the sentence on another sheet of paper.

9.3 **Kirk and I should present the group's report.**
1. What is the verb phrase?   _____
2. Is the possessive noun singular or plural?   _____
3. Which word is a coordinating conjunction?   _____
4. Diagram the sentence on another sheet of paper.

9.4 **Their parents can speak English and Spanish.**
1. Which words are proper nouns?   _____
2. Which word is a helping verb?   _____
3. Which word is a possessive adjective?   _____
4. Diagram the sentence on another sheet of paper.

9.5 **We often walk to the park.**
1. Is the pronoun singular or plural?   _____
2. Which word is an adverb?   _____
3. What is the prepositional phrase?   _____
4. Diagram the sentence on another sheet of paper.

9.6 **Which students have solved the problem correctly?**
1. Is the plural noun regular or irregular?   _____
2. Which word is an interrogative adjective?   _____
3. Is the participle present tense or past tense?   _____
4. Diagram the sentence on another sheet of paper.

9.7 **A pack of wolves howls at the moon.**
1. What is the complete subject?   _____
2. What is the complete predicate?   _____
3. Is *at the moon* an adverb or adjective phrase?   _____
4. Diagram the sentence on another sheet of paper.

9.8 **Hooray! Wednesday is the last day of school.**
1. Which word is an interjection?   _____
2. Which word is a preposition?   _____
3. Which word is an adjective?   _____
4. Diagram the sentence on another sheet of paper.

9.9 **The players on my team are strong and fast.**
1. What is the simple subject?   _____
2. What is the compound subject complement?   _____
3. What is the object of the preposition?   _____
4. Diagram the sentence on another sheet of paper.

9.10 **The kitten is hers, and the hamsters are his.**
1. Which words are possessive pronouns?   _____
2. What is the plural noun?   _____
3. Are the verbs action verbs or being verbs?   _____
4. Diagram the sentence on another sheet of paper.

9.11 **Brad plays baseball, but his brother prefers soccer.**
1. What are the two simple subjects?   _____
2. Which words are verbs?   _____
3. What is the coordinating conjunction?   _____
4. Diagram the sentence on another sheet of paper.

9.1 Subjects, Predicates, Direct Objects, Modifiers

A **diagram** shows how all the words in a sentence fit together. It highlights the most important words in a sentence, and it shows how the other words relate to these important words.

Diagram each sentence.

1. Hawks soar.

2. Spencer drank the juice.

3. A little bird is chirping sweetly.

4. The enormous car stopped quickly.

For additional help, review pages 188–189 in your textbook or visit www.voyagesinenglish.com.

Section 9 • 121

9.2   Indirect Objects

An **indirect object** tells to whom, for whom, to what, or for what the action of a verb is done. In a diagram an indirect object is written on a horizontal line beneath the verb. The indirect object connects to the verb with a slanting line.

Diagram each sentence.

  1. Dad gave Mother flowers.

  2. Al sold his neighbor a bicycle.

  3. His sister bought us a new magazine.

  4. The boy owes his friends some money.

© Loyola Press. Voyages in English   Grade 5

For additional help, review pages 190–191 in your textbook or visit www.voyagesinenglish.com.

9.3 Subject Complements

A **subject complement** follows a linking verb and renames or describes the subject. In a diagram a subject complement is written after the verb. A line that slants to the left separates the subject complement from the verb.

Diagram each sentence.

1. A kangaroo is a mammal.

2. Grapes are a healthy snack.

3. The big dictionary was heavy.

4. My best friend is a fast runner.

For additional help, review pages 192–193 in your textbook or visit www.voyagesinenglish.com.

Section 9 • 123

9.4   Prepositional Phrases

A **prepositional phrase** acts as an adjective when it describes a noun or a pronoun and as an adverb when it describes a verb. In a diagram a prepositional phrase goes beneath the word it describes.

Diagram each sentence.

1. I read a book about bats.

2. The kitten jumped over the box.

3. The frightened puppy was hiding under the bed.

4. A patch of blue sky appeared through the clouds.

For additional help, review pages 194–195 in your textbook or visit www.voyagesinenglish.com.

9.5 Interjections

An **interjection** is a word that expresses strong or sudden emotion. In a diagram an interjection is placed on a line that is separate from the rest of the sentence. The line is above, at the left of, and parallel to the main line.

Diagram each sentence.

1. Ah, I finished my homework.

2. Oh! The problem is difficult.

3. Yikes, he left his backpack in the classroom.

4. Shh! You will scare the timid deer.

For additional help, review pages 196–197 in your textbook or visit www.voyagesinenglish.com.

9.6 Compound Subjects and Predicates

Each part of a **compound subject** or of a **compound predicate** is written on a separate parallel line. The coordinating conjunction is placed on a dashed line between the parallel lines.

Diagram each sentence.

1. Paula and Jim drove to the city.

2. Daniel washed and dried the stack of dishes.

3. Evan or Rodger can bring me the tickets for the concert.

4. The excited baseball fans clapped and cheered.

© Loyola Press. Voyages in English   Grade 5

For additional help, review pages 198–199 in your textbook or visit www.voyagesinenglish.com.

9.7 Compound Direct Objects and Indirect Objects

The parts of a **compound direct object** are written on parallel lines after the verb. The parts of a compound indirect object are written on horizontal lines under the verb. The conjunction on a vertical dashed line connects the parts.

Diagram each sentence.

1. The children made signs and invitations.

2. These colorful birds eat fresh fruit and tasty seeds.

3. Mom gave Isabella and me five dollars for lunch.

4. The principal awarded the older boy and the younger girl a prize.

For additional help, review pages 200–201 in your textbook or visit www.voyagesinenglish.com.

Section 9 • 127

9.8 Compound Subject Complements

The parts of a **compound subject complement** are written on separate parallel lines after the verb. The coordinating conjunction is written on a dashed vertical line between the parts.

Diagram each sentence.

1. His new puppy is soft and cuddly.

2. The last children in line are Susan and her brother.

3. The new soccer coach is strict but fair.

4. My favorite fruits from Hawaii are ripe guavas and juicy pineapples.

© Loyola Press. Voyages in English Grade 5

For additional help, review pages 202–203 in your textbook or visit www.voyagesinenglish.com.

9.9 Compound Sentences

The clauses of a **compound sentence** are written on parallel horizontal lines. Each clause is diagrammed as a separate sentence. The coordinating conjunction on a dashed vertical line connects the clauses at the left edge.

Diagram each sentence.

1. I remembered my homework, but I left my lunch on the counter.

2. Steve's eyes are blue, and Vicki's eyes are deep green.

3. You can open your birthday presents, or we can play some fun games.

4. The dog behind the gate barked fiercely, and we moved away from the rickety fence.

For additional help, review pages 204–205 in your textbook or visit www.voyagesinenglish.com.

Section 9 • 129

9.10 Adverb Clauses

The **adverb clause** is written on a horizontal line under the independent clause and parallel to it. The subordinate conjunction is written on a slanting dashed line that connects the adverb clause to the word it describes.

Diagram each sentence.

1. Until the rain stops, we will postpone our baseball game.

2. When the student finishes his test, he will place it into the basket.

3. Traffic became a mess when snow thickly blanketed the city streets.

4. The large dog ate three biscuits after he raced around the park.

© Loyola Press. Voyages in English **Grade 5**

For additional help, review pages 206–207 in your textbook or visit www.voyagesinenglish.com.

9.11 Diagramming Practice

A diagram shows how all the words in a sentence fit together. It highlights the most important words in a sentence, and it shows how the other words relate to these important words.

Read each diagram and write out the sentence.

1. _____

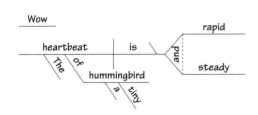

2. _____

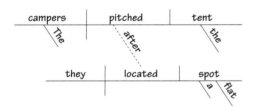

3. _____

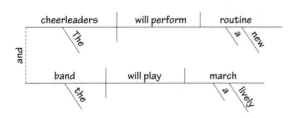

4. _____

_____

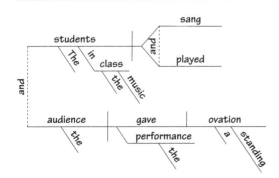

For additional help, review pages 208–209 in your textbook or visit www.voyagesinenglish.com.

Section 9 • 131

What Makes a Good Personal Narrative?

A **personal narrative** tells a story about something that happened to the writer. Personal narratives appear in many kinds of writing, but they all tell about a real experience from the writer's point of view.

Circle the letter of the choice that best completes each sentence.

1. Personal narratives are told

   a. from the writer's point of view.   **c.** in the first-person point of view.

   b. using *I, me, my, our,* and *we.*   **d.** with all of the above.

2. The topic of a personal narrative is

   a. a made-up story about yourself.   **c.** an experience that really happened to you.

   b. always about a lesson learned.   **d.** always about a happy event in your life.

3. A good personal narrative

   a. has many details.   **c.** paints a clear picture for readers.

   b. leaves out unnecessary details.   **d.** is all of the above.

4. The information and language used in a personal narrative

   a. depends on its audience.   **c.** is formal and highly detailed.

   b. is always the same.   **d.** is all of the above.

5. The voice of a personal narrative tells the reader

   a. little about the writer's personality.   **c.** how the writer feels about what happened.

   b. where the writer comes from.   **d.** all of the above.

Rewrite each idea so it is more suitable for a personal narrative.

6. the history of the U.S. flag _____

7. how to care for an iguana _____

8. different types of bicycles _____

Write whether a serious or an excited voice should be used for the topic. Explain your answer.

9. The writer participates in a music competition and wins the grand prize.

   _____

   _____

© Loyola Press. Voyages in English   **Grade 5**

For additional help, review pages 216–219 in your textbook
or visit www.voyagesinenglish.com.

© Loyola Press. Voyages in English   Grade 5

LESSON 2

Introduction, Body, and Conclusion

A personal narrative should have three easily identified parts: an introduction, a body, and a conclusion.

Write *true* or *false* for each statement about personal narratives. Then rewrite each false statement to make it true.

1. The introduction of a personal narrative does not need to grab the reader's attention, but should identify the topic.   _____

   _____

2. The body of a personal narrative has details that tell the story in spatial order.   _____

   _____

3. Do not worry about including too many details. The reader can decide whether or not they are important.   _____

   _____

4. In the conclusion of a personal narrative, the writer can share what he or she may have learned.   _____

   _____

5. Sometimes it is helpful to freewrite about an experience so you can remember all the details about it.   _____

   _____

6. Freewriting words such as *first, next,* and *last* show how events are connected.   _____

   _____

Underline the transition words in the passage. Then write an interesting introduction and conclusion.

_____

First, I left my homework on the kitchen table. After that, I almost missed the bus. For the next hour, I kept feeling like I had forgotten something, but I couldn't remember what. Then it was lunchtime and I remembered. I'd forgotten my lunch! Luckily, my best friend loaned me some money for a hot lunch. _____

_____

For additional help, review pages 220–223 in your textbook or visit www.voyagesinenglish.com.

Sentence Variety

Using different kinds of sentences makes writing more interesting. To add **sentence variety** to your writing, use questions, exclamations, and different word order in sentences.

Rewrite each sentence as a question.

1. I wanted to see a star shoot across the sky.

   _____

2. I've always wanted to go camping in Yosemite.

   _____

3. I remember the first time I hiked Mt. Adams with my family.

   _____

Rewrite each sentence as an exclamation.

4. It's dangerous to swim if there's no lifeguard on duty.

   _____

5. The Grand Canyon is an amazing sight.

   _____

6. Babysitting my younger sister can be a challenge.

   _____

Rewrite each sentence, changing the order of the words to make the sentence more interesting.

7. Terrance jumped after he heard the crash.

   _____

8. We managed to tie off the rope with incredible speed.

   _____

9. Knowing the right codes and passwords is the key to playing the game.

   _____

10. Nobody knew what to do next when the door suddenly slammed shut.

    _____

© Loyola Press. Voyages in English **Grade 5**

For additional help, review pages 224–227 in your textbook or visit www.voyagesinenglish.com.

LESSON
4

Thesaurus

A thesaurus lists synonyms, or words with similar meanings. A thesaurus can help you find the words to say exactly what you mean.

Use the guide words on the dictionary thesaurus pages to write the page on which you would find each word.

1. bored   page _____
2. bent   page _____
3. boast   page _____
4. bird   page _____
5. bright   page _____
6. bleed   page _____
7. bite   page _____
8. blur   page _____

9. trouble   page _____
10. torn   page _____
11. toll   page _____
12. toad   page _____
13. try   page _____
14. tongue   page _____
15. tour   page _____
16. title   page _____

Use this entry from an indexed thesaurus to write the section number on which you would find the synonym for *file* used in each sentence.

file	*noun*:	drawer 247.2
		folder 304.5
		row 522.11
	verb:	to arrange 139.2
		to march 335.47

17. Lisa placed the folders in the *file*.   _____

18. Shane and his classmates formed a single *file*.   _____

19. Please *file* these forms in my desk drawer.   _____

20. The students *filed* into the classroom in a line.   _____

© Loyola Press. Voyages in English   Grade 5

For additional help, review pages 228–231 in your textbook or visit www.voyagesinenglish.com.

Chapter 1 • 135

LESSON
5 Exact Words

> **Exact nouns, adjectives,** and **verbs** give readers the clearest picture with the fewest words. Often one well-chosen word can do the job of many overused words.

Circle the word that is a more exact choice to complete each sentence.

1. "Shh! The baby is finally sleeping," Mom (said   whispered).

2. A (massive   big) bear wandered into our camp last night.

3. Watching the sun set is a (satisfying   good) way to end the day.

4. The wind made the crisp, orange leaves (flutter   move) on the branches.

5. A small (animal   gecko) clinging to the wall startled me.

6. The sergeant (shouted   barked) orders at the bewildered cadets.

7. A herd of horses (trotted   ran) behind the fence alongside the road.

8. Such a low math score left Alicia (sad   disappointed).

9. Kim (stumbled   walked) toward us over the rocky ground.

10. The (conductor   man) in the train's engine waved to the onlookers.

Write a more exact word that can replace the italicized word or words in each sentence.

11. Marla surprises people with her *good* attitude. _____

12. The *article of clothing* in the closet was wet and dirty. _____

13. A *bird* picked its way through the swampy water. _____

14. Sarah *moved* across the room in time to the music. _____

15. The reeds *made a soft noise* as the breeze blew by. _____

16. A lone black cat *went up* to the top of the wall. _____

17. Martin arranged his new *things* on his bedroom shelf. _____

18. The child *came quietly* into the room. _____

19. After the roller-coaster ride, Josh felt *bad*. _____

20. She *laughed* at the silly joke. _____

Use exact words to write a sentence about something you did yesterday.

21. _____

_____

© Loyola Press. Voyages in English   Grade 5

For additional help, review pages 232–235 in your textbook or visit www.voyagesinenglish.com.

LESSON
1

What Makes a Good How-To Article?

A **how-to article** teaches readers how to make or do something. This type of writing has clear, simple steps that are written with a specific audience in mind.

Write *true* or *false* to identify each statement about how-to articles.

1. How-to writing should have a strong, clear topic. _____

2. Writers select how-to topics about which they know little. _____

3. A large amount of detailed information keeps how-to writing interesting. _____

4. How-to writing is the same no matter who or how old your audience is. _____

5. Use imperative sentences in how-to writing. _____

6. Transition words help readers keep track of the steps. _____

Read the how-to article. Then answer the questions.

Did you know that you can train your cat to shake your hand? Cats are very smart and learn quickly. First, get some treats your cat likes. Then put a treat in your hand. Next, hold your hand out to your cat until it reaches up for the treat. Reward your cat with the treat. Repeat this process many times. Soon your cat will reach up to "shake" your hand even without a treat. Cats can learn other tricks too. All it takes is a few treats and some patience.

7. What is the topic of this paragraph?
   a. choosing a cat
   b. training a cat
   c. grooming a cat

8. Who is the audience for this paragraph?
   a. pet groomers
   b. dog trainers
   c. cat lovers

9. How does the introductory sentence grab the reader's attention?

_____

10. What does the writer use to help readers understand and keep track of the steps?

_____

11. Underline the conclusion of the paragraph. What advice does the writer give readers?

_____

For additional help, review pages 254–257 in your textbook or visit www.voyagesinenglish.com.

Chapter 2 • 137

LESSON
2

Order, Accuracy, and Completeness

> To help readers understand a how-to article, it is important for the writing to be **accurate, complete,** and in **logical order.**

Write *1–6* to place each set of directions in logical order. Then write the topic of each set.

1. Put pasta in the boiling water. _____

   Place the pot of water on the stove. _____

   Fill a large pot with water. _____

   Pour cooked pasta into a strainer. _____

   Let the water come to a boil. _____

   Let pasta cook for five minutes. _____

   Topic: _____

2. Save your changes. _____

   Place the cursor where you want to paste the text. _____

   Find the text you want to select. _____

   Cut the highlighted text. _____

   Paste the selected text. _____

   Highlight the text. _____

   Topic: _____

Circle the letter of the direction line in each set that has more accurate information.

3. **a.** Attach the parts with a strong adhesive and allow the parts to dry.
   b. Secure the three dowels with wood glue and let dry for 30 minutes.

4. **a.** In a small dish, mix together 1 teaspoon cinnamon and ½ cup sugar until blended.
   b. Put cinnamon and sugar in a small dish and stir until blended.

5. **a.** Gather the following items: art paper, white glue, scissors, and red glitter.
   b. You will need the following items: paper, glue, scissors, and glitter.

6. **a.** Spread the cream cheese over the ham, roll up, and slice into pieces.
   b. Spread a thin layer of cream cheese on a ham slice, roll up, and cut into spirals.

7. **a.** Heat the milk on the stove, add a lot of cocoa mix, and stir together.
   b. Heat milk over medium heat for 10 minutes, sprinkle cocoa mix over surface, and stir.

8. **a.** Cut the quiche into 8 pieces, and set each piece on a plate with garnish of orange slice.
   b. Cut the quiche into slices, arrange each one on a plate, and garnish.

Write the information that is missing to be able to follow each direction.

9. First, gather the necessary items for the experiment.

   _____

10. Heat oven, set pans in oven, and bake muffins until done.

   _____

For additional help, review pages 258–261 in your textbook or visit www.voyagesinenglish.com.

LESSON
3

Transition Words

> **Transition words** help readers follow the steps in a how-to article. Transition words identify the order of the steps and help carry the reader from one step to the next.

Underline the transition word or words in each sentence.

1. Begin by placing the cardboard on the center of the sheet of paper.

2. The mixture will be runny and pale at first.

3. Now watch carefully for changes in color.

4. Check the temperature of the liquid after 20 minutes.

5. Afterward, the pie should have a golden brown crust.

6. Fold the paper horizontally and then again vertically.

7. Before you start, check that you have all the parts on the list.

8. The next day, check to see if the parts are fully dry.

9. Soon the seeds will send out little white roots.

10. Finally, arrange each section on the page and glue into place.

Write a transition word from the box to make each set of directions clear.

After	After that	Next	Then	First
Finally	To begin	Now	To finish	When you are done

11. _____, start with a wet toothbrush. _____ place a dab of toothpaste on the brush. _____, begin brushing. Brush every tooth well. _____, rinse out your mouth. _____, rinse your toothbrush and put it away.

12. _____, choose the movie you want to see. _____, buy your tickets at the booth. _____ you give your ticket to the attendant, locate the theater where your movie will be shown. _____ find a good seat—not too close and not too far away. _____, sit back and enjoy the movie.

© Loyola Press. Voyages in English   Grade 5

For additional help, review pages 262–265 in your textbook or visit www.voyagesinenglish.com.

Chapter 2 • 139

LESSON
4

Synonyms

Synonyms are words that have the same or almost the same meaning. Writers need to remember that words often have more than one synonym and each synonym has a slightly different meaning.

Write a more interesting synonym from the box for each word.

ecstatic	arrogant	generous	ascend	surly
chortle	mournful	adore	terrified	discover

1. find _____
2. rise _____
3. excited _____
4. sad _____
5. scared _____

6. love _____
7. proud _____
8. giving _____
9. grouchy _____
10. laugh _____

Circle the word in each group that is not a synonym of the other words.

11. small   tiny   little   shallow
12. proper   third   right   correct
13. above   beneath   under   below
14. fragile   delicate   breakable   sturdy
15. method   way   chatter   manner
16. attempt   stop   halt   end
17. go   leave   arrive   depart

Underline the word that best completes each sentence.

18. Everyone agreed that our meal at the Italian restaurant was (superb   good).

19. The game's objective is to (capture   get) the flag from the opponent's territory.

20. The branch blowing against the window made an irritating (noise   rattle).

21. A hungry child (took   snatched) the last roll in the basket.

22. We could tell Kendra was in a good mood as she (moved   skipped) down the sidewalk.

23. The pile of laundry was (large   enormous) and took me the entire day to wash it.

24. "Lunch is ready!" Mom (said   hollered), so we put down our toys and ran inside.

For additional help, review pages 266–269 in your textbook or visit www.voyagesinenglish.com.

© Loyola Press. Voyages in English   Grade 5

LESSON
5

Using the Internet

Using the Internet helps writers find facts for their writing. They know how to check whether this information is **reliable** and **correct.** Knowing the features of the Internet makes using it safer and easier.

Circle the letter of the choice that best completes each sentence.

1. Anyone can set up a Web site ending with the three-letter extension
   a. .org.
   b. .com.
   c. .mil.

2. A search engine
   a. locates Web sites about a topic.
   b. drives the computer.
   c. determines if a Web site is reliable.

3. Keywords help a search engine
   a. locate specific Web sites.
   b. give you a list of vocabulary.
   c. find broad topics.

4. If a Web site has the information you need,
   a. download any linked files.
   b. type in personal information.
   c. check facts against other sources.

Write the words that you could use as keywords for an Internet search to complete each assignment.

5. Design a poster showing and explaining the state flag and bird of Florida

   _____

6. Plan a family trip to learn about the monuments and memorials in our nation's capital.

   _____

7. Find out when and why the bald eagle was removed from the list of endangered species.

   _____

Circle the letter of the three-letter extension that would most likely be at the end of a reliable Web site for information about each topic.

8. the U.S. Navy's achievements during World War II
   a. .mil   b. .com   c. .edu   d. .org

9. a schedule of classes for a community college
   a. .mil   b. .com   c. .edu   d. .gov

10. photographs and descriptions of products on sale at a department store
    a. .com   b. .org   c. .edu   d. .gov

11. where to donate used clothes and household items
    a. .com   b. .org   c. .edu   d. .gov

For additional help, review pages 270–273 in your textbook or visit www.voyagesinenglish.com.

What Makes a Good Business Letter?

A **business letter** is written for a specific purpose to a company, an organization, or a person. Unlike a personal letter, a business letter is formal in tone and sticks closely to a single topic.

Write *true* or *false* to identify each statement about business letters. Rewrite each false statement to make it true.

1. Business letters are written for a specific purpose. _____

   _____

2. A business letter is informal in tone and sticks closely to a few topics. _____

   _____

3. Business letters have different parts to make each one more interesting. _____

   _____

4. Slang and contractions are acceptable in many business letters. _____

   _____

5. Use a polite tone in a business letter to show respect and consideration. _____

   _____

Write a term from the box that matches each description.

heading	inside address	closing	salutation	body	signature

6. _____ This is the part of the letter in which the writers says good-bye to the receiver. It should always be formal.

7. _____ This part includes the receiver's name and job title if you know it, and the company's or organization's address.

8. _____ This is the greeting of the letter and begins with "Dear."

9. _____ Placed in the top left corner of the letter, this includes the writer's return address and the date of the letter below it.

10. _____ This part comes after the closing. It is followed by the writer's printed or typed name.

11. _____ This is the main part of the letter.

For additional help, review pages 292–295 in your textbook or visit www.voyagesinenglish.com.

© Loyola Press. Voyages in English Grade 5

Purpose

When you write a business letter, it's important to state its **purpose** quickly and clearly. There are three common types of business letters: ordering a product, inquiry or request, or a complaint.

Write a word from the box to complete each sentence.

beginning	respond	action	body
clearly	request	ending	information

1. Remember to state the purpose of your letter quickly and _____.

2. Specify what _____ you want the receiver to take.

3. State the purpose of your letter at the _____ of the letter.

4. A business letter should state what _____ you want.

5. The _____ is where you tell the receiver what you want.

6. End a business letter by asking the receiver to act on or _____ to your request.

Write which type of business letter each statement is from: *ordering a product, inquiry or request*, or *complaint*.

7. I was very disappointed when no one could help me at your store on Broadway Street. _____

8. Please send 25 copies of the brochure to the address shown above. _____

9. Because of your experiences in South America and with its many cultures, we would be honored to have you speak at our annual meeting. _____

10. Four of the six glasses shipped to me were broken. _____

11. I would like to know the cost of a new membership and the obligations I would have over the next year. _____

12. I have enclosed eight proof of purchase seals and a check for shipping costs. Please send me one Junior Explorer kit. _____

Write a reason why you might write a business letter.

13. _____

For additional help, review pages 296–299 in your textbook
or visit www.voyagesinenglish.com.

Chapter 3 • 143

Roots

A **root** is a building block for other words. Knowing the meaning of a root can often help you figure out the meaning of an unfamiliar word.

Circle the word that best completes each sentence.

1. The nurse uses a (chronometer   thermometer) to check the boy's temperature.

2. An (autograph   autobiography) is a book a person writes about his or her own life.

3. Her lawyer questioned the (credibility   credit) of the witness.

4. Sarah is a (finale   finalist) in the state music competition.

5. This train will (transport   porter) us to the entrance of the park.

6. He viewed the cells of the plant through the (microscope   telescope).

The Latin root *aqu* means "water." Write the words from the box to answer each question. Use a dictionary if needed.

aqueduct	aquarium	aquifer	aquatic

7. Which word means "growing or living in water"?   _____

8. Which word means "a structure that carries water"?   _____

9. Which word means "a tank of water that contains plants and animals"?   _____

10. Which word means "a wide layer of underground rock that contains water"?   _____

The Greek root *geo* means "earth." Write the words from the box to answer each question. Use a dictionary if needed.

geographer	geologic	geology	geometric

11. Which word means "science of the earth"?   _____

12. Which word means "made up of lines, circles and other simple shapes"?   _____

13. Which word means "a person who is an expert in the study of the earth's surface"?   _____

14. Which word means "of or about geology"?   _____

For additional help, review pages 300–303 in your textbook or visit www.voyagesinenglish.com.

LESSON 4
Combining Sentences and Sentence Parts

Combine sentences and sentence parts to help your writing read more smoothly. **Combine simple sentences** when they are related. **Combine parts of sentences** when they have many repeating words.

Write a new sentence by combining the sentence parts in each pair of sentences.

1. We are making potato salad for the picnic. We are making corn muffins for the picnic.

_____

2. Patricia MacLachlan is a popular author. Louis Sachar is a popular author.

_____

3. At the beach we play volleyball. We swim in the water.

_____

4. Pedro found a biography at the library. Pedro found a book about eagles at the library.

_____

5. Raccoons are nocturnal animals. Hamsters are nocturnal animals.

_____

Circle the conjunction that completes each sentence.

6. The rain poured down on us, (but   or) my new coat kept me dry.

7. We are too late, (but   or) we have arrived very early.

8. We will bring pot roast (or   but) a salad to the potluck dinner.

9. My brother enjoys playing soccer (but   and) basketball on the weekend.

10. Lily wants tuna for dinner, (but   and) her mom is making chicken enchiladas.

Write a simple sentence related to each sentence. Then use both sentences to make one sentence. Use the conjunctions *and, but,* or *or*.

11. Brandon collects old coins. _____

_____

12. Elm Street will be closed on Friday. _____

_____

13. We grew sunflowers in the school garden. _____

_____

© Loyola Press. Voyages in English   Grade 5

For additional help, review pages 304–307 in your textbook or visit www.voyagesinenglish.com.

Business E-Mails

A **business e-mail** follows many of the same rules as for business letters. Even though it is sent electronically, a business e-mail should have a heading, a subject line, a salutation, a body, a closing, a signature, and an address.

Circle the letter of the choice that best completes each sentence.

1. The e-mail address of the person who will receive your e-mail is

   a. the heading.

   b. the subject line.

   c. the salutation.

   d. the closing.

2. When writing the body of an e-mail, be sure to

   a. use abbreviations.

   b. use informal language.

   c. have a beginning, a middle, and an ending.

   d. do all of the above.

3. Just like in a business letter, an e-mail should end with

   a. an address.

   b. a salutation.

   c. your signature.

   d. a heading.

4. Do not open e-mails or e-mail attachments unless

   a. they are mass mailings.

   b. you know the sender.

   c. they ask for personal information.

   d. it looks interesting.

5. Do not unsubscribe from a spam e-mail because the sender

   a. may send you even more spam.

   b. is checking your e-mail address.

   c. will know your address is correct.

   d. will do all of the above.

Write a clear subject line for each business e-mail topic.

6. You want to find out the dates and times of upcoming concerts in the park.

   _____

7. You want to find out how to return a toy that has damaged parts.

   _____

8. You want to find out how to order additional copies of a magazine article.

   _____

For additional help, review pages 308–311 in your textbook or visit www.voyagesinenglish.com.

LESSON
1

What Makes a Good Description?

> An effective **description** paints a picture with words. It makes the reader see and experience a particular person, place, thing, or event.

Circle the letter of the choice that completes each sentence.

1. When you visualize something for a description, think about
   a. how something looks.
   b. how something sounds, smells, tastes and feels.
   c. both of the above.

2. Thinking about the audience who will read your description will help you
   a. find words that are long and complicated.
   b. use words that are appropriate and interesting.
   c. understand the languages that the audience may speak.

3. If your audience already knows a lot about a topic,
   a. you must include as much detail as possible.
   b. you may not need to include basic details about it.
   c. you should not write about it.

4. Using sensory details will help your reader
   a. visualize your topic and share your experience.
   b. understand why you chose to write about the topic.
   c. do both of the above.

Use the description to answer the questions.

> A cool breeze sends showers of brilliant orange and crimson leaves fluttering from gnarled branches. A strong scent of burning leaves accompanies the scent of spicy cinnamon and the crunch of juicy apples. The smooth orange skins of pumpkins signal they are ripe in the field. Piles of brown crispy leaves crackle under the playful romping of children as they play. It must be fall.

5. Circle the sensory details that help describe the setting.

6. Write one detail from the paragraph that appeals to each sense.

   Sight: _____

   Hearing: _____

   Taste: _____

   Touch: _____

   Smell: _____

For additional help, review pages 330–333 in your textbook or visit www.voyagesinenglish.com.

LESSON

2 Ordering a Description

A good description is well organized. The reader is led from detail to detail in a way that makes sense. Two common ways to **order a description** are spatial order and chronological order.

Write whether the organization of each topic's description should be spatial (*S*) or chronological (*C*).

1. Your new bedroom _____
2. Your best friend _____
3. Cooking a special meal _____
4. A favorite movie _____

5. Your cousin's horse _____
6. A trip to an amusement park _____
7. Your pet hamster _____
8. A talent show _____

Cross out the two sentences that are irrelevant to a description of a giant redwood. Then write *1–6* to place the sentences in spatial order from bottom to top.

9. _____ All of us stretched finger to finger couldn't circle the base of the trunk.

10. _____ Indian paintbrush and mountain lily are two kinds of wildflowers here.

11. _____ If I stood on a three-story house's roof, I couldn't have reached the lowest branches.

12. _____ I knew which massive redwood was the tallest before we even got close.

13. _____ The very top was shrouded in a mist and seemed to pierce the clouds.

14. _____ Roots as thick as a person anchored the tree into the spongy ground.

15. _____ Many visitors come to see these giant trees each year.

16. _____ As far as we could see up the trunk, each branch itself was as big as a small tree.

Cross out the sentence that is irrelevant to a description of a mountain hike. Then write *1–7* to place the remaining sentences in chronological order.

17. _____ After we all reached the peak, a chilly rain began to fall.

18. _____ It is important to have the proper clothing and supplies for a hike.

19. _____ The warm sun was on our backs as we started up the rocky mountainside.

20. _____ Even in the cold rain, we stood and marveled at the view.

21. _____ Surrounding the start of the trail were bursts of colorful wildflowers.

22. _____ Joey reached the peak first and gasped at the breathtaking view.

23. _____ We stood there silently for a long time before beginning the climb back down.

24. _____ Halfway up the mountainside, we stopped at a scenic brook to eat lunch.

© Loyola Press. Voyages in English   Grade 5

For additional help, review pages 334–337 in your textbook or visit www.voyagesinenglish.com.

LESSON
3
Graphic Organizers

A **graphic organizer** is a chart or diagram that a writer uses to map out ideas in a visual way.

Use the words from the box to complete each sentence about graphic organizers.

| detail   both   graphic organizer   irrelevant   Venn diagram   word web |

1. A _____ helps a writer map out ideas in a visual way.

2. A _____ organizes details related to a topic.

3. Write each _____ in an oval connected to the chosen topic.

4. A word web can keep you from introducing _____ details.

5. A _____ helps you compare and contrast two topics.

6. The Venn diagram's overlapping part is where you write things that are true of _____ topics.

Complete the Venn diagram by comparing two of your favorite foods.

7.

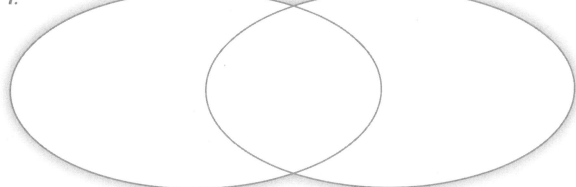

On another sheet of paper, copy this word web. Then add details to it.

My Best Friend

_____

For additional help, review pages 338–341 in your textbook or visit www.voyagesinenglish.com.

LESSON
4

Suffixes

A **suffix** is a syllable or syllables added to the end of a base word to form a new word. Knowing the meanings of suffixes can help you increase your vocabulary.

Write the letter of the definition in Column B that matches each word in Column A.

COLUMN A	COLUMN B
1. activate _____	**a.** cause to be legal
2. personal _____	**b.** to make active
3. legalize _____	**c.** full of fear
4. glorify _____	**d.** capable of being stacked
5. stackable _____	**e.** to make glorious
6. fearful _____	**f.** full of rain
7. rainy _____	**g.** relating to metal
8. metallic _____	**h.** relating to a person

Add a suffix from the box to the word in parentheses to write a word that completes each sentence.

-ify	-ize	-ly	-or	-able	-ful	-ish

9. Thank you for your kind and _____ gift. (thought)

10. Eating a healthy snack will _____ you. (energy)

11. The baby giggles a lot because she is very _____. (tickle)

12. The garden club hopes to _____ the park with those shrubs. (beauty)

13. They found their new neighbors _____ and welcoming. (friend)

14. Michelangelo was a famous _____. (sculpt)

15. That red chair is more _____ than this wooden one. (comfort)

Write a sentence using each word containing a suffix.

16. accidental _____

17. soften _____

18. motivate _____

For additional help, review pages 342–345 in your textbook or visit www.voyagesinenglish.com.

Dictionary

A **dictionary** is a book of words that are listed in alphabetical order. When you look up a word in a dictionary, you find the spelling, the pronunciation, the part of speech, and the definition of that word.

Write _1–5_ to arrange each group of words in alphabetical order.

1. _____ silent _____ sick _____ simple _____ sight _____ sincere
2. _____ crackle _____ crispy _____ creak _____ crack _____ croak
3. _____ brilliant _____ breakfast _____ book _____ bound _____ breathe
4. _____ shower _____ sheep _____ steep _____ spirit _____ squadron
5. _____ under _____ umbrella _____ useful _____ utensil _____ usher

Circle the word or words in each row that would appear on a dictionary page with the given guide words.

6. night • nothing neat nimble nice noise
7. bought • brick break beard bouquet bus
8. cake • careful calm cured capable cable
9. plank • prince plastic pledge princess principal
10. tank • theater target theory tendon thatch
11. intercept • interpret interest Internet intact intern
12. wombat • woolen witness wood women world

Write the letter of the dictionary part that matches each description.

A B C D
re•cite (ri-ˈsit) *v.* **1.** to repeat from memory or read aloud publicly
E
We recite poems for the class. **2.** to relate in full **3.** to repeat or
F
answer questions *-ted, -ting*

13. _____ spelling of last syllable with endings added
14. _____ part of speech
15. _____ definition
16. _____ division into syllables
17. _____ dictionary respelling for pronunciation
18. _____ sample phrase or sentence

© Loyola Press. Voyages in English Grade 5

For additional help, review pages 346–349 in your textbook or visit www.voyagesinenglish.com.

Chapter 4 • 151

What Makes a Good Book Report?

A good **book report** gives information about a book through description, explanation, and example. A book report also gives your personal opinion about the book, stating reasons why you feel as you do.

Write *true* or *false* for each statement about book reports.

1. A book report is an opportunity to tell others about a book you have read.

   _____

2. All characters and settings should be described in detail no matter how unimportant they are.

   _____

3. Most of the book report should summarize the setting.

   _____

4. The plot summary in a book report tells the important parts of the plot but does not give away the ending.

   _____

5. The theme is the message that the author wants readers to get from the book.

   _____

6. Your personal opinion tells whether or not you liked the book and why.

   _____

7. Much of a book report summarizes your opinion.

   _____

Write the letter of the part of a book report from the box that matches each example.

a. character	**b.** setting	**c.** personal opinion	**d.** theme

8. Sometimes those who work the hardest reap the greatest rewards. _____

9. This book has the most fascinating yet frustrating series of events I've ever read. _____

10. I recommend this book to anyone who enjoys Greek mythology. _____

11. Ada and Amy are twins, but that is about the only thing they have in common. Where Ada is cheerful and friendly, Amy distrusts everyone. _____

12. Camp Half-Blood seems like any other summer camp, except the residents there are like no camper or counselor you've ever met. _____

13. It's important to treat others with kindness because someday they may choose to do the same for you. _____

14. Paul has always been a loner, but when he found himself stranded in the wilderness, he realized he'd never been alone like this before. _____

For additional help, review pages 368–371 in your textbook or visit www.voyagesinenglish.com.

© Loyola Press. Voyages in English   Grade 5

LESSON
2

Writing a Book Report

The **information in a book report** should be written in a certain way. Keep the purpose of a book report in mind as you write its introduction, body, and conclusion.

Write yes or no to tell if each item should be included in a book report.

1. the author's name _____
2. the book's ending _____
3. the main characters _____
4. the main events _____
5. contents page _____

6. the theme _____
7. a friend's opinion of the book _____
8. all the characters _____
9. the title _____
10. examples to support your opinion _____

Write a word or phrase from the box to complete each sentence.

plot summary	purpose	introduction	body	author
personal opinion	conclusion	title	theme	setting

11. The _____ of a book report is to share why a book you have read is important to you.

12. The _____ gives more details about the plot and the theme of the book, without giving away the ending.

13. The "life lesson" or general idea of the book is called the _____.

14. The _____ describes the main events in chronological order.

15. Found in the conclusion, the _____ tells how you feel about the book.

16. A book report should include the complete name of the _____.

17. Just like in any type of writing, the _____ gives you a chance to attract the reader's attention.

18. If the _____ is important to the book, describe it in as much detail as the reader will need to understand the story.

19. Underline the _____ or use italics if you are working on a computer.

20. The _____ gives your opinion of the book and includes specific reasons and examples.

For additional help, review pages 372–375 in your textbook or visit www.voyagesinenglish.com.

Chapter 5 • 153

Revising Sentences

A sentence that has too many words or too many ideas is called a **rambling sentence.** A **run-on sentence** is two or more sentences put together without correct punctuation.

Circle the number of each sentence that is a run-on sentence.

1. We found old letters I do not know who they are from.

2. Either Jack or Leah will give the final presentation.

3. Steve swims every day and I like to run but we both like to play volleyball.

4. Madrid is Spain's capital I have never been there have you?

5. I would make a pitcher of lemonade, but we are out of lemons.

6. Myra stayed up late writing and she finished her paper but she left it at home.

Rewrite these sentences. Make shorter sentences or compound sentences. Add correct punctuation and conjunctions or other words where needed.

7. The frightened horses broke free and ran across the pasture they began jumping over the fence and running through the field, it would take a long time to get them back in the stable.

_____

_____

_____

8. In my history class, I learned that Thomas Edison was called the Wizard of Menlo Park he invented or improved many machines and some of these included the telegraph, the telephone, the electric lightbulb, and the typewriter.

_____

_____

_____

9. Even though the rain was pouring down, we continued to play the baseball game, we saw a flash of lightning and the coaches decided to postpone the rest of the game.

_____

_____

_____

For additional help, review pages 376–379 in your textbook or visit www.voyagesinenglish.com.

Prefixes

A **prefix** is a syllable or syllables added to the beginning of a base word that changes the meaning of the word. Knowing what prefixes mean can help you figure out the meaning of new words as you read.

Circle the prefix in each word in Column A. Then write the letter of the definition in Column B that matches each word.

COLUMN A		COLUMN B
1. reheat	_____	**a.** cycle with two wheels
2. multicolored	_____	**b.** having three colors
3. monotone	_____	**c.** not approve
4. uncomfortable	_____	**d.** count wrongly
5. miscount	_____	**e.** heat again
6. bicycle	_____	**f.** a single tone
7. tricolor	_____	**g.** having many colors
8. independent	_____	**h.** not dependent
9. reappear	_____	**i.** view before
10. impossible	_____	**j.** not comfortable
11. preview	_____	**k.** appear again
12. disapprove	_____	**l.** not possible

Complete each sentence by writing a word with a prefix from Column A above.

13. I couldn't sit still because the sofa was very _____.

14. Both France and the United States have _____ flags.

15. Jack was so nervous that he could only speak in a _____ voice.

16. Mia had a flat tire on her _____.

17. It was _____ for us to get to the movie on time.

18. The _____ fabric had all the colors of the rainbow.

19. Just _____ last night's meat loaf for a tasty, hot lunch.

20. My older brother is _____ and lives in his own apartment.

21. The sun began to _____ after the sudden storm.

22. Mrs. Norton was asked to _____ this new book.

© Loyola Press. Voyages in English   Grade 5

For additional help, review pages 380–383 in your textbook or visit www.voyagesinenglish.com.

Chapter 5 • 155

Fact and Opinion

A **fact** is a statement that can be proved true. An **opinion** states a person's judgments or beliefs about a subject. Opinions cannot be proved true or untrue because they reflect a person's feelings.

Write *fact* or *opinion* to identify each statement.

1. This book is a fascinating account of the War of 1812. _____

2. Memorial Day is celebrated in May. _____

3. He was born on May 15, 1993. _____

4. Abraham Lincoln is my favorite president. _____

5. Their new car is candy apple red. _____

6. Ten inches of rain fell in Oregon last month. _____

7. Mr. Jett is a talented painter and sculptor. _____

8. We had a great time on our vacation. _____

9. This movie is a sequel to the one released in 1998. _____

Write *yes* or *no* to identify whether each fact supports the opinion.

10. Africa is a fascinating place to visit.
    It is the world's second largest continent. _____

11. Hawaii has an interesting history.
    People have been coming to these islands for centuries. _____

12. Hummingbirds seem to run on hyperdrive.
    Hummingbirds hover in midair, wings beating up to 90 times per second. _____

13. Kangaroos are unusual animals.
    They are the only large animal to use hopping as a means of locomotion. _____

Underline the word or words that signal an opinion in each sentence.

14. The bravest character in the book was Ramona's brother.

15. My favorite part was when Alfie and his brother locate the treasure.

16. The theme of this book is important to most people's lives.

17. This story is the most suspenseful one I have ever read.

18. The setting was mysterious and set an incredible mood for the story.

19. This fantasy has a more interesting plot than other stories I have read.

For additional help, review pages 384–387 in your textbook or visit www.voyagesinenglish.com.

LESSON
1

What Makes a Good Tall Tale?

A **tall tale** is a story in which the characters, setting, and events are exaggerated. Some tall tales are based on real people like Johnny Appleseed. Others are about made-up characters like Paul Bunyan and Pecos Bill.

Circle the letter of the choice that best completes each sentence.

1. Tall tales feature ___.
   a. a supernatural setting   **b.** a larger-than-life hero   **c.** rhyming dialogue

2. When explaining the plot, a tall tale often uses exaggeration and ___.
   a. persuasion   **b.** statistics   **c.** humor

3. Tall tales often start by telling about the hero's ___.
   a. friends   **b.** future   **c.** childhood

4. Tall tales create surprise by using ___.
   a. exaggeration   **b.** common people   **c.** familiar objects

5. Often a tall tale will explain how ___.
   a. a natural disaster occurred   **b.** some familiar thing began   **c.** a superstition started

6. A tall tale's characters speak in a manner that matches the tale's ___.
   a. time and place   **b.** past and future   **c.** facts and opinions

Imagine a tall-tale character that is the size of your thumb. Describe what each of these objects owned by this character might be or look like.

7. a bed _____

8. a bathtub _____

9. a cup _____

10. a hairbrush _____

11. a ladder _____

Circle *yes* or *no* to identify whether each statement describes a tall-tale hero.

12. The man breathed so deep he inhaled a bird and a couple of butterflies.   yes   no

13. She pulled up a fir tree and used it to comb the tangles from her hair.   yes   no

14. The woman opened her wallet and pulled out two dollars.   yes   no

15. He ate a bowl of soup, a sandwich, and an apple, yet he was still hungry.   yes   no

16. Even three full buckets of water could not quench his thirst.   yes   no

17. When she hollered in California, people could hear her all the way in Florida.   yes   no

© Loyola Press. Voyages in English   Grade 5

For additional help, review pages 406–409 in your textbook or visit www.voyagesinenglish.com.

Chapter 6 • 157

Writing a Tall Tale

Tall-tale writers write about things they know. They use **characters**, **settings**, and **events** that are familiar to them. All tall tales feature a hero that faces a **problem.** The problem's **solution** is often humorous and exaggerated.

Write *true* or *false* for each statement about tall tales.

1. Tall-tale writers choose any subject, even those they know nothing about. _____

2. The first step in writing a tall tale is to choose a hero. _____

3. In a tall tale, the bigger the exaggeration, the more sad the story. _____

4. The hero of a tall tale should have a job the writer knows something about. _____

5. The problem the hero faces should be something that can happen in real life. _____

6. While the rest of a tall tale is humorous, the solution should be serious. _____

7. Superlative adjectives have no use in tall tales. _____

Complete each sentence to exaggerate something about the hero of a tall tale.

8. His mom could hear so well that _____

_____

9. The man slept for such a long time that _____

_____

10. The child ate so many apples that _____

_____

11. The athlete could jump so high that _____

_____

Write an exaggerated solution to each problem.

12. A dam breaks, sending a wall of water crashing down the canyon toward the hero's town.

_____

_____.

13. For weeks the days had been so cold and cloudy that none of the crops were growing.

_____

_____.

© Loyola Press. Voyages in English Grade 5

For additional help, review pages 410–413 in your textbook or visit www.voyagesinenglish.com.

LESSON 3

Figurative Language

Figurative language compares one thing to another in a new and revealing way. **Exaggeration, simile,** and **metaphor** are ways writers use figurative language to make their writing more interesting.

Write *exaggeration, simile,* or *metaphor* to identify the figurative language used in each statement.

1. The day was so hot that tires melted into pools of rubber.   _____

2. Her eyes fluttered like the wings of an overactive butterfly.   _____

3. The sunflower grew to the height of a skyscraper.   _____

4. This steak is as tough as shoe leather.   _____

5. The garage is a maze of tools and car parts.   _____

6. Sonia's smile is a beacon of light on a dark night.   _____

7. He threw the lasso so hard it landed five miles away.   _____

8. The skin on his hands was as rough as sandpaper.   _____

9. I'm so thirsty I could drink up one of the Great Lakes.   _____

10. The closet under the stairs is a black hole.   _____

Write the letter of the choice in Column B that completes the beginning of the simile or metaphor in Column A.

COLUMN A	COLUMN B
11. Icicles hung from the roof, ____	a. like a hot knife cutting butter.
12. The dog's constant bark ____	b. golden honey flowing through the air.
13. His ax cut down the tree ____	c. like busy ants to finish in time.
14. Her lovely voice was ____	d. a ripple of earthquakes as he passed by.
15. The townsfolk worked ____	e. marking the cold like frozen exclamation marks.
16. His heavy steps were ____	f. gouged at the earth like twin steam shovels.
17. The flower garden appeared ____	g. was a jarring alarm that someone was here.
18. The bull's horns ____	h. as though a liquid rainbow had splashed on the petals.

Write a simile and a metaphor to describe two objects in your classroom.

19. _____

20. _____

© Loyola Press. Voyages in English   Grade 5

For additional help, review pages 414–417 in your textbook or visit www.voyagesinenglish.com.

Homophones

Homophones are words that sound alike but have different spellings and meanings.

Circle the homophone for each definition.

1. a basic truth or law   principal   principle
2. to make come apart   break   brake
3. a possessive adjective   there   their
4. to take something and hold onto it by force   seas   seize
5. someone who has the same rank or ability as another person   peer   pier
6. smaller or less important   minor   miner
7. a manner of walking or running   gait   gate
8. a preposition meaning "toward"   too   to
9. to plant seed in   sew   so   sow
10. used oars to move a boat   road   rode   rowed

Circle the homophone that correctly completes each sentence.

11. The miners found a (vein   vain) of gold between the layers of rock.

12. That house at the end of the block is (ours   hours).

13. Ask Vince if he wants to (meat   meet) at the library.

14. Don't forget to (right   write) your name at the top of the paper.

15. A bouquet of lilacs gives a lovely (scent   cent) to a room.

16. This bean dip is (to   too   two) spicy for me.

17. An (or   ore   oar) is a rock that has enough metal in it to make it worth mining.

18. The leaves and berries of the (you   ewe   yew) plant are poisonous.

Write a sentence for each pair of homophones.

19. wood, would _____

20. taut, taught _____

21. ate, eight _____

22. your, you're _____

© Loyola Press. Voyages in English   Grade 5

For additional help, review pages 418–421 in your textbook
or visit www.voyagesinenglish.com.

Nonsense Verse

Nonsense verse is poetry that is completely silly. Writers of nonsense verse dream up weird creatures and unbelievable situations and use rhyme, funny-sounding words, and made-up words to create their poems.

Write a word or phrase from the box to complete each statement.

made-up words	humor	meter	emphasize
couplet	rhyme scheme	syllable	

1. Nonsense verse often uses _____ to entertain the reader.

2. In a _____ each pair of lines rhymes.

3. _____ describes a pattern of stressed syllables in a poem.

4. A _____ is the pattern of lines that rhyme in a poem.

5. In a word with more than one _____, one is stressed more than the others.

6. When we speak, we stress or _____ different words within a sentence.

7. A nonsense poem uses _____, which would not be found in a dictionary.

Mark the syllables in each line of poetry. Then write how many stressed syllables are in each line.

8. All over London the people were laughing.   _____

9. Hiccup, giggle, whisper, hula, moo.   _____

10. Right at the edge of the woods on the trail.   _____

Complete each rhyming couplet.

11. Swirl, twirl, tussle, and skip,
    Stumble, bumble, _____.

12. It leered at me with a gleam in its eye,
    But I was not frightened, _____.

13. Perhaps you met a labrollie today.
    Just what might you do, and _____?

14. She sells seashells,
    But this _____.

For additional help, review pages 422–425 in your textbook or visit www.voyagesinenglish.com.

Chapter 6 • 161

What Makes Good Persuasive Writing?

Persuasive writing tries to make readers agree with a position on a topic. To persuade others to agree with your position, you must present reasons that are supported by evidence.

Circle the letter of the choice that correctly completes each statement.

1. For a persuasive article, the topic should have two
   a. paragraphs.   **b.** opposing views.   **c.** conclusions.

2. The side of the topic the writer chooses is called the
   a. viewpoint.   **b.** introduction.   **c.** reason.

3. In the introduction of a persuasive article, you should grab the reader's attention and
   a. create humor.   **b** state your position.   **c.** summarize your ideas.

4. The body of a persuasive article is where you use details to
   a. convince your audience.   **b.** repeat your position.   **c.** distract the reader.

5. The conclusion to a persuasive article should
   a. share new ideas.   **b.** make the audience angry.   **c.** summarize your ideas.

6. A well-written persuasive article could encourage a reader to
   a. take action.   **b.** stop reading.   **c.** become weak.

Write a reason for and a reason against each position.

7. Students should be able to choose their own school hours.

   _____

   _____

8. Students should be able to wear hats in school.

   _____

   _____

9. Cats are better pets than dogs.

   _____

   _____

10. The community swimming pool should be open for children only one day a week.

   _____

   _____

For additional help, review pages 444–447 in your textbook or visit www.voyagesinenglish.com.

LESSON 2

Writing a Persuasive Article

To begin **writing a persuasive article,** first decide on your topic and the position you will take. Then gather evidence in support of your position and craft it into a clear and convincing article.

Circle whether each statement about writing a persuasive article is true (*T*) or false (*F*).

1. To write a persuasive article, first decide on an audience.   T   F

2. A writer's voice, or tone, is one of the best tools to use in a persuasive article.   T   F

3. Your choice of paper shows that you are confident and that your position and evidence are reasonable.   T   F

4. The audience for a persuasive article is always the same.   T   F

5. Your opinions should be supported by practical, logical ideas and facts.   T   F

Circle the letter of the most persuasive argument in each pair.

6. **a.** A new animal shelter would help the many homeless animals roaming the streets of our city.

   b. A new animal shelter would hold 20 percent more animals and also provide a place for adoption.

7. **a.** A lower speed limit is needed because accidents increased 45 percent when the limit was increased by only 10 miles per hour.

   b. We should lower the speed limit to 55 miles per hour because driving fast is dangerous.

8. **a.** Kids are smarter today than they used to be, so the voting age should be decreased from 18 to 16.

   b. As a result of television and computers, teens are well informed about world events and therefore should be allowed to vote at age 16.

9. **a.** School should start later in the day because most teenagers like to stay up late and, as a result, sleep late in the morning.

   b. Because medical experts have proved that teenagers require more sleep to accommodate rapid growth, school should start later in the morning.

Rewrite each opinion, adding details to make it more persuasive.

10. Dogs are useful to humans.

_____

11. Soccer is good for your health.

_____

For additional help, review pages 448–451 in your textbook or visit www.voyagesinenglish.com.

Expanding Sentences

Good writers vary the length of their sentences. By **expanding sentences** you make them longer, clearer, and more interesting. Use adjectives, adverbs, and prepositional phrases to expand your sentences.

Write adjectives to expand each sentence.

1. Our _____ trip will be to a _____ place.

2. Sarah gave me a _____ painting.

3. My _____ friend sang a _____ song.

4. _____ bears sat under the _____ trees.

Write adverbs to expand each sentence.

5. The young boy _____ whistled.

6. We finished our chores _____ .

7. The crowd clapped _____ and _____ .

8. _____ I fell and _____ scraped my knee.

Write prepositional phrases to expand each sentence.

9. _____ I offered my help gladly.

10. The dog _____ growled and barked at the strangers.

11. We studied for the test _____ .

12. A group _____ walked _____ .

13. The bird _____ sat _____ .

Rewrite each sentence, expanding it by adding adjectives, adverbs, and prepositional phrases.

14. Children are playing.

   _____

15. Bread is baking.

   _____

16. Horses galloped and whinnied.

   _____

© Loyola Press. Voyages in English Grade 5

For additional help, review pages 452–455 in your textbook or visit www.voyagesinenglish.com.

LESSON 4

Antonyms

Antonyms are words that have opposite meanings. Many words have more than one antonym. Words that have more than one meaning might have antonyms for each different meaning.

Write two antonyms for each word.

1. finish _____ _____

2. dry _____ _____

3. soft _____ _____

4. violent _____ _____

5. quiet _____ _____

6. gloomy _____ _____

7. generous _____ _____

8. terrible _____ _____

Circle the three antonyms for the italicized word in each row.

9. *strong*	weak	sorry	flimsy	powerful	sturdy	fragile
10. *give*	provide	share	take	grab	seize	thank
11. *bottom*	under	summit	behind	top	restore	peak
12. *identical*	same	different	varied	twin	diverse	solid
13. *empty*	bare	full	hollow	occupied	packed	hungry
14. *common*	unique	familiar	original	usual	rare	ordinary

Write an antonym that can replace the italicized word in each sentence.

15. The math test yesterday was *difficult*. _____

16. The child recited the poem in her *loudest* voice. _____

17. His new bus pass is *temporary*. _____

18. This puzzle is too *difficult* for me. _____

19. Manny's *elaborate* scheme was a good idea. _____

20. The movie's plot was *interesting*. _____

21. This apple is too *sour*. _____

22. We thought the painting was *ordinary*. _____

For additional help, review pages 456–459 in your textbook or visit www.voyagesinenglish.com.

Library

No matter how large or small, all **libraries** use special systems to organize their resources and make information easy to find. Knowing how to use these systems can help you find the book or information you are looking for.

Write whether each book would be found in the *fiction*, *nonfiction*, or *reference* section of a library.

1. *Ramona the Pest* by Beverly Cleary _____

2. *Webster's New World Student's Dictionary* _____

3. *Romeo and Juliet* by William Shakespeare _____

4. *Facts about Arabian Horses* by Jenna Sherrill _____

5. *Great Battles of World War II* by Dale Lerner _____

6. *World Atlas* _____

7. *Where the Red Fern Grows* by Wilson Rawls _____

8. *Farmer's Almanac* _____

Write *true* or *false* for each statement about computer catalogs.

9. A computer catalog is not easy to use. _____

10. Computer catalogs have entries listed only by title and author. _____

11. When you type a word into the search box, the computer will give you a choice of entries. _____

12. Today most libraries have their catalogs on computer. _____

Write whether you would use the *title*, *author*, or *subject* for each of the following to find a book in the library.

13. books about endangered species _____

14. latest book in the series by Rick Riordan _____

15. *Maniac Magee* _____

16. kid-friendly recipes _____

17. books by Lois Lowry _____

18. *Coral Reefs: In Danger* _____

19. simple machines and how they work _____

20. nonfiction books about ants _____

For additional help, review pages 460–463 in your textbook or visit www.voyagesinenglish.com.

LESSON
1

What Makes a Good Research Report?

A **research report** is a kind of writing that tells readers factual information about a topic in an organized way. A research report shares ideas that a writer has read and collected from a variety of sources.

Write the letter of the choice in Column B that completes each sentence in Column A.

COLUMN A

1. The topic of a research report ____

2. The purpose of a research report is to ____

3. Because a report will reflect your interest and enthusiasm, ____

4. Use questions as you do research to ____

5. Information for your report can ____

6. Develop a topic sentence to help you ____

7. An effective introduction ____

8. A good conclusion ____

COLUMN B

a. choose a topic that interests you.

b. catches the reader's attention.

c. give factual, organized information about a topic.

d. may be your choice or chosen for you.

e. guide your research.

f. summarizes the topic of the report.

g. come from a variety of sources, such as books, reference materials, and Web sites.

h. help you decide which information is important and which is not.

Circle the letter of the choice that is the narrower topic for a research report.

9. **a.** the city of Brazil   **b.** cities of South America

10. **a.** ocean mammals   **b.** toothed whales

11. **a.** expeditions to the South Pole   **b.** Ernest Shackleton's South Pole journey

12. **a.** natural disasters   **b.** how to prepare for an earthquake

Write two details that support each topic sentence. Do research if needed.

13. The platypus is a unique kind of mammal.

   a. _____

   b. _____

14. Paul Revere played an important role in the American Revolution.

   a. _____

   b. _____

15. An ants' nest is a complex habitat.

   a. _____

   b. _____

For additional help, review pages 482–485 in your textbook or visit www.voyagesinenglish.com.

Gathering and Organizing Information

You will need to **gather and organize information** for a research report. Taking notes in an organized manner will help you sort your information and properly credit the sources you use.

Write a word from the box to complete each sentence.

end	articles	index	bottom	brackets
source	notes	cards	author	underlined

1. A book's _____ can help you see if there is information related to your topic.

2. To take _____, write in your own words the information you find.

3. A handy way to take notes is to use note _____.

4. For each piece of information, write the name of the source, the author, and the page number at the _____ of the card.

5. The Works Cited page is found at the _____ of a report.

6. Each entry of a Works Cited page is a _____ used in your report.

7. The titles of books are _____.

8. The titles of _____ are put between quotation marks.

9. For Web site sources, put the address between angle _____.

10. If a Web site does not give the _____, begin the entry with the name of the article.

Write whether each source from a Works Cited page is for a *book*, an *encyclopedia*, or a *Web site*.

11. "Beavers." World Book. 2010 ed. _____

12. Afar, Matt. Mushrooms. Portland: Timber Press, 2009. _____

13. Murray, Seth. Manatees. Orlando: Tiptop Publishing, 2010. _____

14. "Time Line of Inventions." 3 April 2011 <www.timeforall.org> _____

15. "Hurricanes." Encyclopaedia Britannica. 2008 ed. _____

16. "Earthquake Hazards." 25 January 2010 <earthquake.usgs.gov> _____

17. Sanchez, Ana. Africa. New York: Penguin Books, 2010. _____

For additional help, review pages 486–489 in your textbook or visit www.voyagesinenglish.com.

© Loyola Press. Voyages in English   Grade 5

LESSON
3

Outlines

An effective way to organize information for a research report is to write an **outline.** An outline helps you decide which information you want to use and how to present that information in an order your readers can follow.

Rewrite each false statement about outlines so it is true.

1. An outline can be used as the final form of a report.

   _____

2. An outline is like the heart of a research report.

   _____

3. Main ideas are labeled with capital letters.

   _____

4. Each main idea will become a separate page in a research report.

   _____

5. Because an outline is not part of the final report, it does not need to be neat.

   _____

6. The ideas in an outline can be a mix of sentences, phrases, and words.

   _____

Write three details for each main idea in the outline. Do research if needed.

7. Types of Rocks

   I. Igneous rocks

      A. _____

      B. _____

      C. _____

   II. Sedimentary rocks

      A. _____

      B. _____

      C. _____

   III. Metamorphic rocks

      A. _____

      B. _____

      C. _____

For additional help, review pages 490–493 in your textbook or visit www.voyagesinenglish.com.

Compound Words

Compound words are two words joined together to form one word. Recognizing the two words that make up a compound word can help you figure out its meaning.

Write a word in Column B to complete each compound word in Column A.

COLUMN A		COLUMN B
1. fire_____		head
2. head_____		body
3. arrow_____		light
4. sun_____		plane
5. every_____		place
6. air_____		rise

Complete each sentence with a compound word from above.

7. Our _____ was delayed due to the weather.

8. Sam placed several logs in the _____.

9. Our class took a vote, and _____ voted to play soccer.

10. The car's _____ was broken in the accident.

11. Dad woke us up early so we could watch the _____.

12. A hiker found a Native American _____ by the creek.

Write two compound words that contain each word.

13. bed   _____   _____

14. thunder   _____   _____

15. water   _____   _____

16. news   _____   _____

17. coat   _____   _____

18. fire   _____   _____

19. school   _____   _____

20. book   _____   _____

21. rain   _____   _____

© Loyola Press. Voyages in English   Grade 5

For additional help, review pages 494–497 in your textbook or visit www.voyagesinenglish.com.

Library Reference Materials

Reference books and materials give information and facts about a wide variety of topics. These resources are kept in the reference section of the library and cannot be checked out. Each reference book has a special purpose.

Write a word from the box to complete each sentence.

| reference | index | keywords | atlas |
| almanac | periodicals | articles | encyclopedia |

1. An _____ is a reference source that contains articles about people, places, things, and events.

2. The _____ section of a library contains books that each have a special purpose and that cannot be checked out.

3. An _____ contains maps that may show geographical features, political features, historic locations, climates, and populations.

4. The _____ in an encyclopedia often include diagrams, pictures, and maps.

5. An _____ contains very recent facts and statistics and is published every year.

6. Magazines are called _____ because they are published periodically. They provide up-to-date information.

7. Information in older issues of periodicals can be found by using an _____.

8. Using _____ related to your topic can help you locate information in various sources.

Write whether you would use an *encyclopedia*, an *atlas*, or an *almanac* to find information on each topic.

9. the history of the transcontinental railroad _____

10. the three longest bridges in the United States _____

11. the names of five different types of conifers _____

12. the interstate highways through Rhode Island _____

13. the months with the least amount of rainfall in Georgia _____

14. the names of three islands in the South Pacific _____

For additional help, review pages 498–501 in your textbook or visit www.voyagesinenglish.com.

Chapter 8 • 171